THE NARCISSISM RECOVERY WORKBOOK

SKILLS FOR HEALING FROM EMOTIONAL ABUSE

Brenda Stephens, MS, LPCC

ROCKRIDGE
PRESS

For general information on our other products and services or to obtain technical support, please contact our Customer Care Department within the United States at (866) 744-2665, or outside the United States at (510) 253-0500.

Rockridge Press publishes its books in a variety of electronic and print formats. Some content that appears in print may not be available in electronic books, and vice versa.

TRADEMARKS: Rockridge Press and the Rockridge Press logo are trademarks or registered trademarks of Callisto Media Inc. and/or its affiliates, in the United States and other countries, and may not be used without written permission. All other trademarks are the property of their respective owners. Rockridge Press is not associated with any product or vendor mentioned in this book.

Interior and Cover Designer: Carlos Esparza
Art Producer: Hannah Dickerson
Editor: Adrian Potts
Production Editor: Nora Milman
Production Manager: Michael Kay

Cover illustration used under license from iStock.com

Author photo courtesy of Matthew Burd

Paperback ISBN: 978-1-64876-471-4
eBook ISBN: 978-1-64876-472-1

R0

THE NARCISSISM
RECOVERY WORKBOOK

To my children, Elissa and Ian, you are my everything.

Contents

Introduction

I would like to welcome you to this workbook. It takes courage to face painful experiences, and I hope that you'll take a moment to be proud of your choice to start your recovery.

My name is Brenda Stephens, and I am a licensed clinical counselor who has helped many clients on their journey in recovering from narcissistic abuse. I also train other therapists to recognize and understand this unique and insidious type of abuse. This book draws from my professional knowledge as well as my own experience in relationships with narcissists, which I talk more about on page 27.

Most likely, when you have tried to explain the abusive behavior you have endured with the narcissist in your life, it's hard to express the nuances of their disrespectful and abusive treatment. This lack of understanding and awareness by others can leave you feeling alone and unsupported. Without the help from someone who has lived through narcissistic abuse themselves, your journey toward recovery might feel like a lonely, difficult pursuit. This book is intended to show you that you are not alone. Many people have experienced narcissistic abuse and thankfully, more people are starting to grasp what it is.

We are beginning to understand that narcissism runs on a spectrum. We have a better understanding that there are covert narcissists, who seem shy or self-deprecating—traits we would not think would apply to someone with narcissistic tendencies. We're also recognizing that narcissists can hold positions in the community that appear to be selfless or charitable, but are actually motivated by a need for attention and praise. When you are in a personal, romantic, familial, or professional relationship with a narcissist, you see the real person.

This book will help you discover that it's not necessary for other people to see the narcissist in your life the same way you see them. You'll learn to radically accept that the narcissist will do whatever they must do to find their audience of admirers and will likely move from person to person, social circle to social circle, as they find new sources of supply of attention, burn them out, then move on again.

This workbook is designed to help you understand what a narcissist is, the differences between different types of narcissists, and how they got to be the way they are. You'll be able to identify the vulnerabilities you carry that have made you a target to a narcissist. Those of us who have been in relationships with narcissists often discover that we have had more than one in our life, like we have a magnetic draw to them, or them to us. We often feel that we are more sensitive or empathic than others, which can seem like a beacon that draws a narcissist to us.

Through the exercises and practices in this book, you'll learn to build effective boundaries, care for yourself, and learn to trust your instincts when the wrong person tries to enter your life. You will learn that the boundaries you set for yourself are the strongest tool you will have in creating and maintaining healthy relationships.

Recovering from narcissistic abuse is both challenging and possible. We can feel so overwhelmed and upside down in even understanding what has happened after experiencing a relationship with a narcissist that the path to recovering can seem unclear and difficult to navigate. This workbook can help you make sense of what you have encountered, build the resilience and self-love to heal from narcissistic abuse, and take proactive steps to avoid falling into a relationship with a narcissist ever again.

In conjunction with using this workbook, I strongly encourage you to seek out therapy, psychiatric care, support groups, or other resources to help navigate your recovery process. There is a growing number of mental health providers who are starting to recognize and treat people who suffer this unique type of abuse. Most mental health providers want to make sure they're the right fit for you, so don't be afraid to ask prospective providers if they understand this type of abuse in order to find the right person to guide you through your journey.

PART ONE

Understanding Narcissism

There is a lot of talk about narcissism today. Many people use the term loosely to describe anyone who exhibits selfish behavior, but what is narcissism, really? Numerous professionals in the mental health field recognize that narcissism exists on a spectrum. Despite the term being thrown around casually, true narcissism is rather rare. One key characteristic of truly narcissistic behavior is lack of empathy. Someone can be selfish and still have empathy for others, but a narcissist will manipulate to get what they want without concern about who they hurt in the process. The lack of empathy is what leaves those of us with empathy turned upside down and wondering what happened. We just do not think that way. Understanding this difference in thinking will help in the process of healing and taking steps toward recovery.

CHAPTER 1

What Is Narcissism?

In this chapter, we will explore what narcissism is to provide a foundation from which to start the recovery process. We'll look at where the term "narcissist" originated in Greek mythology. We'll also look at what narcissism looks like in modern times, and what it is and is not. We'll explore how the narcissist affects those around them. You'll learn how to recognize the red flags before you get in too deep with the narcissist. You will understand how the narcissist leaves you feeling following interactions with them and why. Finally, we'll explore how to start the recovery process.

REAL-LIFE STORY: MATT

Matt came to me as he was starting the divorce process with his wife. He was filled with sadness, and as he began to reflect on his wife's narcissistic tendencies, he realized that his mother exhibited all the same traits. Matt was devastated that his marriage had turned out the way it did and that his sons were so influenced by his wife's tyrannical and self-serving behaviors.

As Matt went through the process of trying to protect his sons, he recognized how much of his own childhood he was seeing repeated with his sons. This awareness allowed Matt to understand what his children were going through, giving him unique insight into how to help them mend. Matt was also able to recognize his own unhealed childhood wounds and went through his own recovery process alongside his children. He discovered that there was a sad, lonely little boy still living within him. He attended therapy, did a great deal of reading, and found ways to support his sons by simply giving them love and his undivided attention. Matt has done a lot of work toward healing and is now helping others as they find their own way to recover and thrive after a relationship with a narcissist.

What Does It Mean to Be a Narcissist?

There are clinical descriptions of narcissism, but the word is often used too casually. Selfishness does not make someone a narcissist, but when they have little concern for others and put themselves before everyone else, that is more on the narcissistic spectrum.

There are healthy areas of narcissism in a mild form, such as feeling pride and telling others about an accomplishment to share the joy and receive well-earned praise. This is different from bragging about something with a stance of superiority and putting others down.

The clinical definition of narcissistic personality disorder as defined in the DSM-5 (*Diagnostic and Statistical Manual of Mental Disorders*) states that a narcissist has at least five of the following nine traits:

1. A grandiose sense of self-importance

2. Preoccupation with fantasies of unlimited success, power, brilliance, beauty, or ideal love

3. Belief that they are "special" and unique, and can only be understood by or should associate with other special or high-status people or institutions

4. Need for excessive admiration

5. Sense of entitlement

6. Interpersonally exploitative (takes advantage of others)

7. Lack of empathy

8. Envy of others or belief that others are envious of them

9. Shows arrogant, haughty behaviors and attitudes

Although these are clinical definitions and five of nine need to be met for diagnosis, people who have only some of these characteristics or demonstrate them only on occasion can be just as damaging to others. This is what we mean when we say that narcissism can be found on a spectrum. Whether diagnosable or low on the spectrum, narcissists will bring emotional chaos into your life. What is common to every narcissist is a lack of empathy, no matter where they fall on the spectrum. They are selfish, self-serving, manipulative, dishonest, and conniving. They take no responsibility for the awful things they do to people and blame others for all the chaos and pain they create.

When Did the Term Originate?

The term "narcissism" comes from the Greek myth, defined in a poem written in 8 CE, of a young man named Narcissus who rejected the women who fell in love with him and reacted to them with disdain. After witnessing his contempt toward his admirers, the goddess of revenge, Nemesis, cursed Narcissus after leading him to a pool of water, where he saw his own reflection and fell in love. Narcissus withered away gazing at his own reflection and died at the pool of water.

Narcissism in Modern Life

Narcissism in modern life is as dramatic as the story of Narcissus but plays out differently. Although some children are overindulged and fawned over, leading them toward a narcissism similar to that of Narcissus, others gain narcissistic traits through abuse, neglect, and trauma. Today, narcissists have ample opportunity to gain admirers in a world where appearance, wealth, and showmanship are often valued. Social media has allowed narcissists access to a wider audience. For those with an insatiable need to be admired and build a following, our Internet-connected world is fertile ground. Once, a narcissist's reach only went so far. Now narcissists are becoming more familiar to us, and many more of us are feeling the pain they cause.

Common Signs of Narcissism

There are many behaviors that narcissists are capable of; however, there is much commonality in the way they all seem to operate. I often tell my clients who seek support from narcissistic abuse that it's as if they all have a shared playbook, because they all seem to act out in such similar ways. Here are some of the most common signs:

Lack of empathy: Narcissists do not seem to have the capacity to care about others the way most people do.

Lack of accountability: A narcissist is skilled at turning the tables and not being responsible for anything that goes wrong. They can even be manipulative enough to have us apologizing for the chaos and abuse that they cause.

Aversion to shame: This aversion is so strong that it drives most of their other behavior. Because a narcissist has no developed ego (sense of self), their sense of self is derived from what is reflected back to them from others. If the narcissist is met with shame, they are destroyed. Shame causes pain to the part of the narcissist that they are always desperately trying to hide. This pain is utterly intolerable and often leads to narcissistic rage.

Lying: To keep their charade going and avoid being exposed, the narcissist is a master at lying. Their lying gets so mixed up with their own truth it often seems that they, themselves, do not know the difference between their fabrications and reality.

Among Family and Friends

Family members may have the toughest time understanding that their family member is a narcissist because, to them, this may be something they are accustomed to. If the narcissist is a parent or a sibling, the family has probably tolerated their behavior from the beginning and might not even know that it is abnormal. The narcissist has a tough time maintaining lasting friendships, and the friends they do keep are manipulated and often end up doing the narcissist's bidding as an extension of the narcissist, perhaps reaching out to victims to relay messages or trying to bully or guilt the victim into speaking with the narcissist after they have gone no-contact (page 62).

In Romantic Relationships

In a romantic relationship, the narcissist creates a picture of fairy-tale love and convinces the object of their desire that the two are meant for each other—twin flames, soul mates. This can be music to the ears of the person hearing these words, and the narcissist knows it. This is called "love bombing" and the narcissist moves quickly in this stage, even saying "I love you" unusually early in the relationship. The narcissist turns up the charm, then inevitably shifts gears and "turns" on the recipient of that charming behavior. Slowly, the outbursts and abuse become more frequent and insidious, leaving the romantic partner confused, lost, and hurt.

At Work

Narcissists in the workplace have their own special wickedness because they're in direct competition with people around them. Instead of creating a peaceful workplace, they are always looking to one-up their coworkers, throw them under the bus, and take credit for others' work. If the narcissist is your boss, this can be particularly unpleasant due to the power they have and the lengths they will go to maintain that power.

Interesting Statistics on Narcissism

According to the DSM-5, about 6.2 percent of people in the United States meet the diagnostic criteria for narcissistic personality disorder and up to 75 percent of them are men. These numbers are slowly changing to reflect more women being diagnosed, but the vast majority are male.

Narcissists are drawn to careers that keep them in high esteem, such as doctors, politicians, military officials, police officers, and firefighters. Narcissists often have other disorders as well. Some of the most common co-occurring disorders are depression and anxiety, along with substance use disorders. This is not surprising given that so many narcissists become that way, in part, because of abusive and/or neglectful childhood relationships with caregivers.

Research conducted at the University of Chicago Medicine is shedding light on the biological causes of narcissism. Researchers are finding evidence that there is a hypersensitivity in interpersonal relationships that narcissists cannot tolerate. This early research leads to some understanding that both nurture and nature likely lead to this disorder (Nature vs. Nurture, page 15).

What Does It Mean to Have Been a Victim of a Narcissist?

To have been a victim of narcissistic abuse is devastating. Most of us do not figure out what the problem is with the narcissist in our lives before investing a lot of time and energy in them in some way. Whether the narcissist is at work or at home, it is not obvious right away that the person in question has narcissistic traits, and they tend to cause a lot of emotional damage before we figure it out. In the workplace, we may be trying to gain the approval of a boss who is constantly raising expectations. With a parent, we are trying to gain love, nurturing, and attention and learn what works to get those needs met. This leaves a developing child incapable of knowing what a healthy relationship looks like. In a romantic relationship, we so want to believe in the flowery picture the narcissist has painted for us that we tend to find ways to justify their behavior even when the behavior is overtly toxic. In any case, the non-narcissist is usually bewildered and needs time to understand and heal from what happened to them.

Anxiety

Victims of narcissistic abuse tend to live in a state of constant anxiety. They have learned to walk on eggshells and will go to great lengths to keep the peace. This often means that they neglect their own wants and needs to focus on keeping the narcissist happy. These people are constantly on high alert, worried that something will go wrong.

Confusion

Being in the company of a narcissist will leave anyone confused. The narcissist spends their time negating the reality of those who are close to them. They blame others for hurtful things they have done or said. You may have found yourself apologizing for not reacting the way they wanted you to—regarding something *they* did.

Shame

Shame is a theme that runs through every bit of a narcissistic relationship. The narcissist lives through the lens of shame and makes sure that those around them do as well. Narcissists have high expectations and are constantly raising those expectations. Your inability to meet them due to this ever-changing standard is not because there is something deficient in you; it is the narcissist's way of making sure they keep you "in your place" by shaming you for not being "good enough." None of us will ever live up to these expectations because the narcissist will never be satisfied.

Self-Doubt

As you might be starting to see, it is the narcissist's goal to make you question the way you view the world and fall in line with their way of thinking. The shame and manipulation a narcissist uses to gain control leave you doubting all that you know, and ultimately succumbing to and deferring to them. They will convince you that you have made so many mistakes and they know what is best, and you will start to believe it because they break you down slowly. This is what makes narcissistic abuse so insidious.

PTSD and Complex PTSD

Post-traumatic stress disorder, PTSD, is a diagnosis in the mental health and medical fields. It's diagnosed as a result of an experienced or witnessed traumatic event. Most people who have suffered narcissistic abuse have what is commonly known as C-PTSD, or complex PTSD. With C-PTSD, there is not always just one defining trauma. C-PTSD is like a brick wall under construction. Each brick represents a trauma, and one is piled on top of another, leaving the individual with this overwhelming burden.

Other symptoms of narcissistic abuse often include:

- Isolation (this helps the narcissist maintain control)

- Depression (living like this can feel hopeless)

- Inability to make decisions (you no longer trust yourself to know what is right)

- Enabling (to keep the peace, you are always there to respond to their needs)

- Fear (eventually you see the world as being unsafe)

- Lack of sleep (anxiety and fear make it impossible to sleep soundly)

Emotional Abuse Can Have Long-Term Effects

So much damage is caused by the stress and anxiety that come with abuse of any kind. In fact, research is showing there is not much difference in how the brain and body react to physical or emotional abuse. In children, it is common to see some regressive behaviors (returning to thumb-sucking, bedwetting, etc.). In adults, we see behaviors such as substance abuse, attachment to toxic friends and partners, chronic pain, and eating disorders, to name a few.

We are continually learning about the mind/body connection and how constant stress damages physical functioning. People with a history of abuse will often have digestive issues, fibromyalgia, chronic headaches and migraines, and problems with memory (because the brain can be ineffective at accurately forming new memory connections after trauma).

Self-Assessment:
Your Experience with a Narcissist

Take a moment to answer "yes" or "no" to the following questions and consider your experiences in relation to each one.

Have you found yourself giving up friendships or reducing time with friends?	YES	NO
Do you or did you look forward to times when your narcissist was at work, out of town, or otherwise away from you?	YES	NO
Have you noticed physical symptoms like headaches or stomach pains when you knew you would be interacting with the narcissist in your life?	YES	NO
Do you find yourself using cruel or derogatory language in your self-talk?	YES	NO
Do you feel drained, confused, or exhausted after a phone call or time spent with the narcissist in your life?	YES	NO
Are you overly justifying decisions you have made?	YES	NO
Are you finding yourself unable to recall conversations you have had with your narcissist?	YES	NO
Do you notice yourself feeling inadequate or incapable?	YES	NO

Please reflect on your answers to these questions. If you answered "yes" to any, ask yourself: Is this what you believe or are these lies someone told you about who you are?

This Book Will Help You Start the Healing Process

You're here and that's good, because understanding what has happened is the first step to healing. No matter what your experience has been, ultimately the narcissist wants control and admiration, and as you start to recognize the tools and manipulation they use to meet these needs, you get to decide where your boundaries need to be so you are no longer wrapped up in their twisted behavior. Recognizing how bad things have gotten over time within your relationship with a narcissist can be shocking, but hopefully also validating. Many of us blame ourselves for not seeing what was happening with the narcissist, but now you see it, and from here you will come to understand your own vulnerability and how to recover and heal.

Conclusion

In my work with survivors of narcissistic abuse, I've seen a common thread of self-blame and minimization of how harmful the abuse actually was. It is similar to that old saying: If you throw a frog into a pot of boiling water it will jump out, but if it is lukewarm water and you turn the heat up slowly, the frog stays right where it is. This is often the type of thinking that many of us get caught up in and before we know it, we can no longer stand the heat but don't know what to do. The narcissist seems to know the right thing to say and do to get the attention of their next victim. They seem to be attracted to people who have a lot of empathy, compassion, and kindness.

So many of the clients who come to me for therapy blame themselves for falling for the narcissist's tricks and games. You are not to blame! Narcissistic behavior is not something most of us understand or expect to encounter, and it is not abusive all the time, which allows us to believe that the ugly behavior is not the "real" person. We want to believe that they are the charming person they seemed to be when we first met them.

It cannot be stressed enough how important it is to have support from people who really understand narcissistic abuse during the recovery and healing process. There are more and more therapists who understand this type of abuse, and even social media groups can help you feel supported and understood. The Resources (page 126) in this book can also help you find support and create a plan to remove yourself from the abusive relationship.

In the next chapter, we'll take a closer look at what makes the narcissist behave the way they do and how they have honed their skills to hide who they really are. You'll gain a deeper understanding of the different types of narcissists and why they can be dangerous people to be around.

CHAPTER 2

Uncovering the Narcissist

In this chapter, we will take a deeper look into what narcissism looks like in the day-to-day world. It will give you a better understanding of the different types of narcissists and what makes them tick. This deeper understanding is also a way to start your own healing process, as you begin to see that the emotions you have been feeling are what the narcissist wanted you to feel in order to maintain control. This chapter will help you see narcissism for what it is and recognize that none of what you have experienced—whether it's feeling like you're going crazy, less confident, depressed, or isolated—is a reflection of you.

REAL-LIFE STORY: KAYLA

A client, Kayla, came to me a few years ago feeling desperate about her marriage and not knowing what to do about the way she was being treated by her husband, Chris. After years of gaslighting (an emotional abuse tactic that makes the receiver doubt their perception of reality), insults, lies, and vague threats, Kayla had reached a new low. She and their son were in an automobile accident, and instead of being concerned about the injuries she and her son sustained, he admonished her for getting in the accident and totaling the car. Chris told family members and friends that Kayla caused this accident and he would no longer let her drive any of his three vehicles, even though they had four children under the age of 10 who needed rides to school.

After doing a little research on abuse and recognizing that Chris's behavior was narcissistic, Kayla realized that she needed to get a divorce but was afraid of being a single parent and what it would mean for her financially. Eventually, she realized that living without the daily abuse was worth the risk. After getting some therapy and understanding what it meant to be married to and parent with a narcissist, she was able to set firm boundaries and leave the relationship.

Narcissism Is on a Spectrum

Although certain criteria need to be met to be for a diagnosis of narcissistic personality disorder (NPD), most experts familiar with this disorder recognize that it presents on a spectrum. People who meet all diagnosable criteria would be high on the spectrum; however, a narcissistic person can show some empathy or accept someone else's success without being jealous. Most people do have some level of narcissism, which can help us reach goals and desires. When the narcissism becomes harmful to relationships, work life, or leaves the narcissist with no other notable personality traits, we see it as unhealthy and disordered. Even with diagnosable traits of narcissism, we can see varying levels of severity. Remember that one needs to show at least five of the nine criteria to be diagnosed with narcissism (page 4). Which of those criteria are met can make the difference in how a person presents under the umbrella of narcissism.

The Benefits of Healthy Narcissism

There are healthy narcissistic traits, as long as they are in line with the greater good for the person and society. Healthy narcissism is a bit like healthy self-esteem. It can be felt when you have faced a particularly difficult challenge and conquered it or when you have pride or joy in something you created or accomplished. Healthy narcissistic traits can help us build self-esteem and confidence to challenge our self-imposed limits so we can reach goals and make our wishes come true.

Nature vs. Nurture

There is still so much to learn about how narcissistic personality disorder (NPD) starts, but some evidence suggests that there may be a genetic component. Previously, it was believed that the environment in which a child was raised was the path to NPD, whether it involved overly praising and indulging a child, or abusing or neglecting a child. There is now evidence that the chance of being a narcissist is greater if you have a narcissistic parent. It is difficult to discern whether that is because narcissism was modeled by the parent or if it's the result of gene expression. Not all children of narcissists become narcissists, but we do not know why, scientifically. Like a lot of things, narcissism is likely a result of both nature and nurture.

When Narcissism Becomes Dangerous

Any involvement with a narcissist is dangerous on some level. Even a casual relationship can leave you confused and questioning yourself, but a more intense or involved relationship comes with many risks. If they get their way, a narcissist will eventually have you feeling like there is something wrong with you and that you are not attractive, smart, or worthy enough. The more time spent in a relationship with a narcissist, the more you lose who you really are and start believing the version of yourself that they have projected onto you. Eventually, you feel as though you are going crazy because your reality and perception of things have been dismissed so consistently. In a long-term relationship with a narcissist, your true self gets increasingly hidden away until you almost do not recognize yourself. This is intentional because the narcissist wants people to doubt you and wants to isolate you, so they keep control and power as the person you spend all your time, energy, and attention on. They cannot bear to be second to anyone.

A Small Percentage of the Population Is Diagnosed with Narcissistic Personality Disorder (NPD)

According to the DSM-5, about 6.2 percent of the population in the United States meet the criteria for diagnosis of NPD. Of that 6.2 percent, it is estimated that up to 75 percent are male. The number of narcissists is increasing and there are more women estimated to have this disorder than ever before. It's unclear whether people are becoming more narcissistic because of social media or if they just now have a platform that increases their reach so we are seeing it more. More research is needed.

Covert vs. Overt Narcissism

With narcissism, we often see some distinct differences between overt and covert narcissists. The overt (also known as malignant) narcissist tends to show traits that we expect, possessing a lack of empathy and overdeveloped sense of self-importance. They are manipulative, deceitful, and obvious in their pursuit of attention and admiration. They tend to be charming and often work in "helping" careers.

A covert narcissist looks very different. They are harder to spot, less obvious in their attempts at getting attention, and can appear vulnerable and introverted. As with overt narcissists, covert narcissists are unable to accept criticism and have a sense of entitlement and grandiosity—they're just quiet about it. They will blame their inability to succeed on some outside source or some perceived injustice.

Both types of narcissists share similar traits such as selfishness, manipulation, and lack of empathy, to name a few. I'm often asked which type is worse. I believe they are both destructive and leave those around them negatively affected, just in different ways.

A Narcissist Has Many Goals

Narcissists start to learn their "skills" when they are young. By their late teen to early adult years, they have developed seriously maladaptive behavior and, as they get older, they learn to hone their behavior to be more efficient at getting their needs met. With experience in different types of relationships, narcissists learn what works and doesn't work in getting the attention and admiration they crave. They typically have mastered the art of manipulation and wearing the mask of confidence, gregariousness, and charm to win over their victims.

They have little to no sense of who they are and can only build a sense of self by what is reflected back to them through the eyes of others. This works for them when their targets are buying into their charm, but this never lasts in the consistent, unquestioning way that the narcissist needs it to so they can feel normal. This is where all the conflict comes in. We grow tired of their games, but they frantically need our admiration—we'll explore how.

Boost Self-Importance

A narcissist will present to others an image of themselves being the best at a sport, the smartest in the room, or the most desired for their looks. They need to feel superior to others to fill the void of their own lack of self-esteem. Their view of themselves lives only in how impressed others are with them.

Be the Center of Attention

Whether overt or covert, the narcissist needs to be the center of attention. If they are not, they have effectively disappeared. They cannot tolerate being alone with their thoughts for long. Providing them with the center of attention is similar to giving water to a person stranded in the desert. They will drink it up quickly and need more immediately to carry on.

Collect Praise and Compliments

Social media is a good example of the importance to the narcissist of collecting praise and compliments. The narcissist will post on social media so they can keep track of all the likes and attention they get. They will typically post themselves doing something exciting or seemingly altruistic and check back often to bask in the glow of the feedback they receive.

Elevate Themselves over Others

The narcissist needs to feel that they are the best, because for someone else to be better, to them, means being the worst. Their lack of emotional maturity leaves them looking at the world as all or nothing. If someone is better than they are at something, the narcissist is destroyed; therefore, they present themselves with an air of superiority. They will dismiss any evidence of being bested by attributing it to cheating, unfairness, or someone "out to get them," to convince themselves that they are better than everyone else.

Create Confusion and Self-Doubt in Their Victims

This is one of the most insidious things a narcissist does. Through gaslighting and lies, the narcissist will do anything to avoid taking blame or accountability. They will get caught up in details to sidetrack any communication that might lead to them being revealed and seen in a negative light. They are vague and lie by omission, and they will twist things around so you don't even remember what you were discussing in the first place. Their goal is to have you questioning your own perception of reality so they can maintain control and have you deferring to their way of seeing things.

Manipulation

A narcissist will use manipulation to get their victims to do something for them or behave in a way that benefits them. They will use your feelings of guilt or compassion to pay their debts or get them out of other trouble. They might isolate you from your family and friends so your attention is not given to anyone else. They will tell you part of a story so if it ever gets back to you, they can say they already told you about the incident in question. They are calculating and intentional in their manipulation.

Withhold Affection and Intimacy

It is common for a narcissist to be withholding and emotionally distant, even with basic affection such as hugging their children or holding hands with their partner. A narcissist in a romantic relationship will often withhold sexual intimacy or be emotionally disconnected when intimate with their partner. It may be too vulnerable for them to show affection, and withholding can be a way to maintain power.

Create Dependency

Another common goal of a narcissist is to create codependency. After being worn down, the target of their abuse may often forgo their own concerns, desires, and needs in order to keep the peace in the relationship. This self-sacrifice leaves them feeling unsure of themself and, over time, reliant on their partner. While it may seem incongruent for a narcissist to be dependent on another, they rely on the admiration of their partner in order to strengthen their fractured ego (sense of self-esteem or self-importance). This dynamic creates a codependence that works in favor of the narcissist to retain power and control in the relationship.

Statistics on Male and Female Narcissists

Although the percentage of the population that meets the diagnostic criteria for narcissistic personality disorder is low, there is quite a difference in the numbers of male versus female narcissists. According to a study published in *The Journal of Clinical Psychiatry*, 7.7 percent of men and 4.8 percent of women fit the diagnostic criteria—a large difference given the small numbers in each category. The difference they found is that men have higher levels of envy and lack of empathy than women, but more research is needed to uncover other differences.

Your Experience with a Narcissist: You Deserve Validation and Support

Because people do not understand the intricacies and insidiousness of the narcissist's behavior, it's easy to feel unsupported and unheard. Thankfully, there seems to be an increase in the understanding of narcissistic abuse. Support groups, social media groups, and therapists like myself who specialize in treating victims of narcissistic abuse are becoming more prevalent. There are books, videos, and articles to validate you and help you further understand what you have been through (see Resources, page 126). Those feelings that something was not quite right were correct. Your intuition was telling you something, but you couldn't hear it clearly because your narcissist was louder. Hearing the stories and experiences of others can be incredibly validating, and it is possible now to find others who understand you.

Recovery Will Take Hard Work and Perseverance

Just like any significant change we try to make in life, recovery from any toxic relationship takes some work. I can assure you that it will be so very worth it. After you have moved past the clouded, foggy thinking you experienced in your relationship with a narcissist, you'll be happy that you persevered and got through it. So many people I work with have questioned whether they should just suffer through because it's easier than making big life changes, especially if the narcissist is your spouse and a parent of your children, or the one signing your paycheck. Even if the narcissist in your life is a parent or sibling and you are an adult, a lot of healing needs to take place. If you have gone no-contact with your narcissist, it is important to take time to do the work of learning how to love and respect yourself, so you never again sacrifice who you are in order to gain love and respect. It is most important to take the time to figure out who you are and what's important to you. The narcissist has chipped away at your identity to increase your dependence on them, and part of the recovery process is getting that identity back.

Your Healing Is Worth It

Whether you've had a long-term relationship or a short one with a narcissist, you are probably left reeling from all the emotional upheaval and mental games. Just imagine what it will feel like to not live in confusion and to make decisions that you want to make. To be able to have a conversation with someone who listens to, and cares about, what you have to say. To spend time exploring what gives you joy, and saying "no" to things that do not sit well with you. There is a peaceful future waiting for you and a rediscovery of yourself that you get to take all the time you want to explore. One of the most important things I hope you'll get familiar with in your healing is your intuition. We seem to lose that connection to our gut reactions, and regaining that skill is important to prevent falling for the charms of a narcissist in the future.

A Mindful Meditation for Difficult Times

You don't need any special knowledge, unique clothes, or fancy pillows to meditate. You can do it anywhere, anytime. The goal of meditation is to gain control over your thoughts and remain in the present.

1. Find a comfortable, quiet place to sit (chair, floor, bed, desk).
2. Take a moment to scan your body and notice if you are holding tension anywhere. Focus on this tension, wherever it is, and take a moment to stretch out the tense area and relax.
3. Close your eyes or soften your gaze and focus on your breath. Notice the rise and fall of your chest as you breathe in and then release your breath in a long exhale. Try exhaling as if you were blowing through a straw to help you fully release your breath.

4. If you notice your thoughts straying away from your breath, simply notice that without judgment and bring your attention back to your breath.

Meditation sounds easy, but it can take a little practice. Be kind with yourself. Start your meditation practice slowly by sitting in meditation for as little as a minute at a time, then increase your time as you continue your practice.

Conclusion

There is a significant difference between someone behaving in a selfish manner and someone who is truly narcissistic. It's important to recognize that narcissistic traits are seriously harmful and more than just being self-centered. I hope that you can see the lengths to which a narcissist will go to get their needs met, even if it means sabotaging the mental health of another, and that living with this kind of abuse takes its toll. The good news is that recovery is possible, and reclaiming your identity is a journey that will help you heal, learn to love yourself, and trust your instincts in the future. In part 2 of this book, you'll find exercises and practices to help you understand your experience with a narcissist, along with tools to create boundaries and skills to nurture healthy relationships in the future.

PART TWO

The Stages of Recovery

It's time to focus on recovery and reclaiming freedom from abusive relationships. You'll find exercises to help you recover and practices and prompts to keep you on the right track, loving and caring about yourself. We'll explore real-life stories of people who have been in your shoes so you can see that you're not alone. From the stories of those who have healed and moved on, I hope you'll see the promise of a life waiting for you to come live it on your terms.

CHAPTER 3

Start with Acknowledgment and Acceptance

In this chapter, you will learn skills and gain tools to recognize and repair the damage caused by your relationship with a narcissist. Two of the most important things you can do for the foundation of your recovery are: Acknowledge what you have experienced and accept that this is truth. The acknowledgment and acceptance will help you move from the "if only" way of thinking (wishing things were different, such as "if only I had left earlier") into action toward recovery by accepting things as they are. By using the activities in this chapter, you will start to process what you have experienced and truly understand the control and manipulation that have been imposed upon you.

REAL-LIFE STORY: ANA

My client, Ana, was married to her narcissistic husband for 13 years and was convinced by him that the problems in their marriage were all due to her not being a good wife and mother. As Ana started to heal through therapy and support groups, she started to acknowledge that her husband was indeed verbally, emotionally, and sometimes physically abusive. Eventually, she was also able to accept that what drove his behavior was narcissism. Initially, she wanted to believe that there was a part of him that had compassion and empathy, but as she saw his actions toward their children becoming more unkind as they got older, she was able to radically accept that he was not who she hoped he could be.

As she got to the point of acknowledgment and acceptance, she was able to create and maintain boundaries for herself, which ultimately meant no longer accepting his mistreatment of her or the children. She started focusing her attention on her healthy friendships and family relationships and nurtured them to create a strong support system. This system supported her as she ended her marriage and worked on rebuilding her own identity and thriving in life instead of just surviving.

Radically Accepting Where You Are

Radical acceptance is a complete acknowledgment of reality as it is, without assigning judgment. It involves letting go of wishing that things were different and any bitterness or bargaining in your mind (for example, "If only I hadn't argued so much, we could have gotten along better"). This acceptance and can be hard to embrace but is crucial in order for you to recover.

Please take a moment to reflect and write down where you feel you are in your recovery process and where you would like to be. This will help you stop fighting the past, as you take an honest look at where you are now, what you are feeling, and what will be the first steps in feeling better.

Write a statement about how you are feeling about yourself (pleased, lacking confidence, etc.):

_____

_____

_____

Write a statement about how you would like to feel about yourself (accepting, loving, confident, etc.):

_____

_____

_____

Speaking from Experience

I understand, from experience, how important it is to do this work for yourself. I have been in two relationships with narcissists—one overt (malignant) and one covert, and was too young and in love (with the covert one) to see things clearly. The covert narcissist has stayed in my life for several years because of our children, so I speak from experience on how important it is to trust your intuition and have strong boundaries—two of the key skills we'll explore in these chapters. As someone who's "been there," I encourage you to take time for all the exercises, prompts, and practices in these upcoming chapters. Some of them may be uncomfortable at first but as you lean into them, you'll learn so much about yourself and your power within. You are building a toolkit for taking control of your life.

Take Inventory

As we start looking at the recovery process, it's a good idea to take inventory of our own vulnerabilities, so we know how to set goals for ourselves. Please look at the following list and put a check mark next to the statements that seem to fit with your experience.

☐ I feel the need to accomplish things to feel worthy of love.

☐ I feel guilty if I say "no" to someone's request.

☐ I am generally suspicious of people.

☐ I have never understood what it means to love and accept myself unconditionally.

☐ I find it difficult to treat myself with kindness.

☐ I have no recollection of feeling whole or complete.

☐ I have not been able to sit still without thinking that I should be doing something.

☐ I am not able to accept compliments easily.

☐ I am my own worst critic.

Start by taking the two or three statements that resonate with you most and use them for your first round of goal-setting. Focusing on two or three goals is manageable and leads to the best chances of success.

Create Goals for Recovery

Let's take the statements you chose from the checklist in the previous exercise and create goals using those statements as a guide. For example, if you chose the statement "I feel guilty if I say 'no' to someone's request," a simple, manageable, and achievable goal could be something like "I will take time to check in with myself before saying 'yes' when someone requests something of me."

If you can relate to the statement "I find it difficult to treat myself with kindness," a goal could be "When I catch myself using negative self-talk, I will stop, and I will say one kind statement to myself." These kind statements can be along the lines of forgiveness, such as "Everyone makes mistakes" or "I am worthy of love no matter what." Small goals can lead to significant changes as you go through the healing and recovery process.

Goal 1:

_____

_____

_____

Goal 2:

_____

_____

_____

Goal 3:

_____

_____

_____

How to Create Objectives to Reach Your Goals

For each goal that you created in the previous exercise, let's figure out some objectives to help you reach those goals. Using the example goal from the previous exercise, "I will check in with myself before saying 'yes' when someone requests something from me," you can create a plan for how to reach that overall goal. For this goal, your objective might be "I want to become more aware of my reactions to requests" or "I want to learn to trust my instincts when making decisions."

Please take two goals from your list and create objectives for each of them. Keep it simple to start—you can always explore this more deeply as you go. In exercise 4, we'll add another step to break things down even further so you can start working on these first steps to recovery right away. Breaking down goals into manageable tasks makes them more achievable.

Objective 1:

_____

_____

_____

Objective 2:

_____

_____

_____

Objective 3:

_____

_____

_____

Track Your Success

Before moving on to the next exercise, consider setting up a calendar to help you track your successes. Changes are made by taking small, simple steps toward your goals, and keeping track of those steps can encourage you to keep going. A simple "yes" or "no" on your calendar can help you recognize how often you have been taking time to work on your goals.

How to Create Interventions to Reach Your Objectives

Interventions are steps you take to work toward your objectives, which will help you meet your goals. This is where the work is, and it can be life-changing. Using our examples from the previous exercises, let's create some interventions.

For the objective "I want to become more aware of my reactions to requests," interventions can be "I will take 10 seconds after receiving a request to check in to see if there is tension anywhere in my body." Another intervention can be "I will respond to the request by saying 'I need time to think about this and get back to you.'" Giving yourself permission to take time to consider what is best for you is also a great start to the art of setting up boundaries, which we'll address later.

Intervention 1:

_____

_____

_____

Intervention 2:

_____

_____

_____

Intervention 3:

_____

_____

_____

Take a Moment to Care for Yourself

You should be very proud—the exercises you have completed up to this point are some of the hardest you will do in this book. Let's take a moment for you to write some positive statements about yourself. They don't need to be elaborate. It could be something like "I have had the courage to face with acceptance that I have been in an abusive relationship and I am now motivated to make change." Write two or three thoughts that are meaningful to you and then come back to this prompt often to reassure yourself.

Positive statement 1:

_____

_____

_____

Positive statement 2:

_____

_____

_____

Positive statement 3:

_____

_____

_____

Learning to Leave the Land of "What If"s

Many of us spend a lot of time trying to make sense of what happened. We ask ourselves whether we could have done something different to keep the relationship from getting toxic or if only we could have been more patient. The best thing we can do for ourselves is shake the fog in our brains that a narcissistic relationship creates, accept that it was not what we wanted it to be, and move forward.

Please take some time to write down your "what if" thoughts, then write a response challenging that way of thinking.

For example: "What if I had been more understanding and patient?"

Challenge: "I was more patient than I should have been, even to the point of enabling the behavior, which was harmful to my own mental health."

What if:

_____

_____

_____

Challenge:

_____

_____

_____

_____

What if:

_____

_____

_____

Challenge:

_____

_____

_____

_____

What if:

_____

_____

_____

Challenge:

_____

_____

_____

_____

Cognitive Distortions

In this exercise, please take some time to note the good and bad times in the relationship. Recognizing that not every moment was horrible in this relationship leads to the foggy thinking mentioned in the previous exercise. If we take stock of the good times versus the bad, I am guessing that the bad happened more often, which incongruently makes us romanticize the good times into something they were not. This is called cognitive distortion. We are so desperate for those good moments that we excuse a lot of bad behavior. If you are no longer with your narcissist, clinging to the few good memories as something worth having can put you at risk of returning to the toxic relationship or obsessing over getting it back.

GOOD TIMES   BAD TIMES

_____   _____

_____   _____

_____   _____

_____   _____

_____   _____

_____   _____

_____   _____

_____   _____

_____   _____

Gratitude Meditation

Let us now take a few minutes to note the things in our lives that we are grateful for. This exercise is good to do daily, especially as you start your day. It can make all the difference in how you set the tone for your day. When done before bedtime, it can make for a more restful night of sleep:

1. Sit or lie in a quiet, comfortable space.

2. Close your eyes or soften your gaze.

3. Think of three things you are grateful for—anything from your morning coffee to the home you live in. Reflect on each thing for the good feelings it generates.

I hope you never run out of things for which you are grateful. As you picture each thing, allow a smile to come to your face in appreciation of the object of your gratitude. This will improve mindfulness of the small things and the important people who surround us.

Don't Go Down the Rabbit Hole of the Past

It's easy to replay the interactions with your narcissist over and over in your mind, trying to make sense of what will never make sense. We can lose hours a day replaying events in our minds. When you find yourself going down that rabbit hole, stop yourself, forgive yourself, then do this exercise. This effective exercise can help you stay present in the current moment.

Take note of five things you can see: _____,

_____, _____,

_____, _____,

Take note of four things you can feel: _____,

_____, _____,

_____

Take note of three things you can hear: _____,

_____, _____

Take note of two things you can smell: _____,

_____

Take note of one thing you can taste or like the taste of: _____

_____

List the People in Your Support Group

Therapists often have clients make crisis plans when the client is in an abusive relationship. Whether you are still in the relationship or have separated, having support around you is essential. We sometimes forget to reach out when we most need to. Please list at least two people you can reach out to when you are feeling overwhelmed. List more if you have more, and don't be discouraged if you have only one. The narcissist works hard to alienate you from others and may have caused you to lose relationships with friends and family. Don't judge yourself. Even if it's a crisis hotline for when your emotions overwhelm you, write down the numbers so you can call or text when you are suffering.

Contact #1:

_____

_____

Contact #2:

_____

_____

Get Back in Touch with Who You Are

Toxic relationships, like a relationship with a narcissist, put us in survival mode. We spend a lot of time trying to keep the narcissist content and forget about our own needs. As you heal and reclaim your identity, get in touch with yourself so you can turn to interests and hobbies as you recover, instead of focusing on the relationship. Make a list of things that spark your interest or that you used to do to with your free time. This can be playing an instrument, charity work, gardening, reading, spending time with a pet, etc. The possibilities are endless, and rediscovering, or discovering for the first time, something you love is invigorating and leads to a renewed sense of self.

List your interests and hobbies here:

_____

_____

_____

_____

_____

_____

_____

Removing Shame: A Letter to Your Future Self

As we transition into the next chapter, my hope is that we can start getting some of the shame you might feel out of the way and start focusing on all the greatness that is you! Shame is poison to the spirit of who we are. It is toxic and often undeserved, but time spent with a narcissist creates a lot of shame as they break you down and keep you down. Shame is a feeling of being a bad person or being undeserving or unlovable. Keeping you feeling this way keeps the narcissist in control. An opposite feeling of shame can be openness. In this exercise, I challenge you to tell your story in the form of a letter to your future self. You don't have to share it with anyone—simply writing out your story will be a step toward healing. Please use the space below to openly and honestly write a letter to your future self, explaining your experience with your narcissist and the role you played in staying in the relationship. Be careful not to blame yourself; simply be honest about the relationship as a whole and take pride that you have decided to recover and heal. If you need more space, feel free to write this letter in a journal or notebook.

_____

_____

_____

_____

_____

_____

_____

REAL-LIFE STORY: BRIDGET AND VIKTOR

Bridget came to therapy heartbroken that her ex-husband was seeing someone romantically. Even though they had gone through a divorce, Bridget and her ex-husband, Viktor, were still speaking of reconciliation. When he started dating, she was convinced that if only she tried harder or consented to his wishes, he would not have found someone new. As Bridget started to recognize Viktor's constant criticism and insults, she recalled that this was similar to how her mother behaved during Bridget's childhood.

By taking inventory of her own history, she was able to make connections to how she was reliving her childhood with Viktor, then learned how to recognize that her negative self-talk and need to be productive were vestiges from her childhood. She realized that she transferred these behaviors to her relationship with Viktor because this pattern of behavior was familiar to her. As Bridget began to recover and learned to establish boundaries and speak to herself kindly, she discovered that Viktor's rejection was a gift to her, as she finally possessed self-acceptance and a sense of peace in her life.

Support: Staying on Track with Acknowledgment and Acceptance

Recovery from narcissistic abuse can feel like a lonely journey. When you connect with others who have had a similar experience, it can feel incredibly validating. These connections can also keep you on track in your healing and recovery and stop you from falling back into any cognitive distortions. Your support system can help you look at your history with clear vision and maintain acceptance and acknowledgment.

When you become confused in your recollection about, let's say, what good deed your narcissistic sister did once, it can reduce confusion when you're surrounded by support. This will remind you that she did it for praise and admiration, not from the goodness of her heart. There are many more opportunities to find support for this type of abuse than ever before. Many practices, including my own, offer support groups that help with staying present in acknowledgment and acceptance and not falling back into distorted ways of thinking.

Conclusion

In this chapter, we've looked at the first steps toward healing. We must recognize and accept what has happened before we can start making changes, so we never again find ourselves in a toxic relationship. I hope you will look back through your responses to the exercises and take pride in how far you have come. It takes courage to look so closely at ourselves. On a deeper level, it might help you recognize additional areas for growth and healing, because there may be hidden wounds from earlier in life that led you to be vulnerable to toxic relationships. If you come to this realization, I hope you will consider getting additional help to work through this.

In the next chapter, we'll start doing the important work of learning to love and accept ourselves. I assure you that when you embrace self-love and acceptance, you'll see the world in an entirely different light and be able to experience life much more fully.

CHAPTER 4

Boost Your Self-Love, Self-Compassion, and Self-Esteem

In this chapter, we'll get to the heart of healing from the insidious emotional abuse that you have likely suffered. Arguably, the two most important changes to make toward healing are learning to love and accept yourself as you are and trusting your instincts. After a relationship with a narcissist, we are beaten down and have lost connection with our core self because of the lies the narcissist has told us about ourselves. As you learn to show yourself love and respect, you will begin to trust your emotions and reactions and not dismiss them because they are inconvenient for the narcissist. You'll pay attention to that knot in your stomach when something doesn't feel right and trust that it's warning you to protect yourself from potential harm.

REAL-LIFE STORY: JULIAN

My client Julian has been on a path of healing and self-discovery since before he began therapy a couple of years ago. The transformation has been uplifting to watch, after he learned more about the intergenerational trauma of having a narcissistic father, then marrying a narcissist, which destroyed him. He was so busy trying to keep the peace with his father and his wife that he had no energy to consider the pain he was in. As with nearly all my clients, the feeling that he was "going crazy" led him to research what it was about these two relationships that was so similar and destructive. Julian realized that both his father and his wife had significant narcissistic traits, so he sought therapy.

Julian did exercises and practices similar to those in this book and learned volumes about himself. Most importantly, he learned that when alarm bells are going off in his body (often called a gut reaction, or in his case, sensation in his arms), he needs to take stock of what is happening and reassess before moving forward. He also began learning to honor himself, and as he did this, love began to exude from him for himself, his children, and others. He chose to let honest, loving people into his life and let go of the toxic relationships.

Tune In to Your Feelings

Please take a moment to briefly check in with what you may be feeling. Simply notice if reading the story of Julian ignited any feelings for you, either physically or emotionally. Write down your feelings, then relate what you are feeling to the goals you identified in the beginning of the book (page 28). Use this prompt when you notice other feelings to see if they are in alignment with your goals.

_____

_____

_____

_____

_____

_____

_____

Listen to Your Body

Learning to trust your gut or other physical reactions is essential to getting in touch with and caring for your core self.

1. Lie down or sit comfortably with your feet firmly on the floor.

2. Starting from the top of your head, imagine a healing light working its way from your head to your neck, then shoulders.

3. Take time to recognize where there may be tension and notice it, then relax the muscles related to that tension (unclench your jaw, release your shoulders).

4. Release tense muscles as you work down through your torso, hips, arms, legs, and feet.

Doing this practice daily will help you relax and get in touch with your body and what it is already telling you.

Basic Self-Love

Learning to love ourselves starts with basics. Depending on how hectic your life is, or how much anxiety and stress (or other emotions) you experience, you may be ignoring some key elements of caring for yourself. I have seen clients forget to get enough nutrition, hydration, and rest. Use the table on page 46 to log when you are doing these basic self-care tasks—a simple "yes" or "no" in the corresponding box is sufficient. This log will help you identify where you might be neglecting yourself so you can take small steps to change.

	ADEQUATE HYDRATION	AT LEAST ONE HEALTHY MEAL	RESTFUL SLEEP
Monday			
Tuesday			
Wednesday			
Thursday			
Friday			
Saturday			
Sunday			

A Deeper Look at Self-Care

Self-care seems to be at the front of the minds of a lot of people, and there are items you can buy or spa days you can plan that might make you feel better, but self-care can be so much simpler. Paying attention to the little things our minds and bodies need might be all we need to do, and that doesn't cost us anything.

Of course it's nice to treat yourself, but it's also beautiful to know yourself well. Does being around people drain your energy? Do you need time to unwind by yourself after a day at work? Do you prefer to be around a lot of people to feel energized? These are just a few examples, but they and other preferences are crucial to living your best life. As a therapist, I know that after a day at work I have to leave the heaviness of my profession in the office and take some time to myself for quietness before I have the energy to fully engage in my family life. Knowing your preferences is an intuitive way to show yourself kindness, respect, and love.

The Core Self

The difference between an introvert and an extrovert boils down to where they draw energy from. Answer the following questions to see which you identify with most. When you know how you prefer to interact with others and spend your time, you can create opportunities to honor who you are.

Please put a check mark next to the characteristics that resonate with you.

Introvert characteristics:

☐ I prefer to take time to think before making a decision.

☐ I prefer spending time in thought than in extended conversations.

☐ I need time to recharge after social interactions.

☐ I prefer to interact with one or two others than be in a crowd.

☐ I feel reserved unless I know someone well.

☐ I prefer facts over lofty ideas.

☐ I prefer not to take risks.

Extrovert characteristics:

☐ I make decisions without exploring consequences.

☐ I feel energized in social situations and seek them out.

☐ I am comfortable speaking in groups.

☐ I am motivated by reward.

☐ I am open with strangers and acquaintances.

☐ I like being the center of attention.

☐ I engage in risky behaviors.

These are not exhaustive lists of either personality type, but by answering these questions, you can start to get an idea of where you fit. I invite you to explore what it means to be an introvert or extrovert to help with better self-understanding in the next prompt.

Reflect on What You Have Learned about Yourself

After you take the quiz on the previous page, I invite you to reflect on what you have discovered. Differing personality styles between you and the narcissist can explain a lot about how you communicate and interact. If, for example, you know that a phone call or other interaction with your narcissist is likely to drain your energy, you can create boundaries around how long you will interact with them. If you have a coworker who is narcissistic and uses up your entire break time telling you all about their most recent achievement, you can let them know you have only five minutes to talk before getting back to work, instead of letting them abuse your time. Please take a moment to note how you can create boundaries to respect your own needs.

_____

_____

_____

_____

_____

_____

_____

_____

_____

_____

_____

_____

_____

Knowing It Is Not about You

Given that many narcissists are extroverts, it is interesting to notice how these personality traits play a role in who they are and may have even been what attracted you to this person in the first place. It can also be true in the reverse. Covert narcissists may lean more toward introverted characteristics. These traits can cause conflict whether this is a family member, a romantic partner, or a coworker.

Knowing your own preferences is important, as is understanding the demands the narcissist might have based on their personality characteristics. The more you understand that a narcissist behaves in ways that serve them, the less you will blame yourself for the chaos that happens and recognize that much of this, while directed at you, has nothing at all to do with who you are. That's when you can really step back and decide to protect yourself.

Put Your Introvert or Extrovert Tendencies to Work for You

Now that you have a better idea of where you lean on the introvert or extrovert spectrum, let's explore ways to honor and protect your needs. Note that having introvert tendencies does not mean you never like to socialize, nor does having extrovert tendencies mean you never want to be alone. Most of us land somewhere in between.

Whether you identify as more of an introvert or extrovert, it is essential to honor your need to recharge your energy and take time for recovery. On page 50, please write down a few ways that you notice your energy is depleted, then write down how you can counteract that depletion. For example, as an extrovert, you might find your energy drained because you haven't been able to spend time with friends. A solution could be putting boundaries on work or caretaking, so you have more time for friends.

ENERGY-DRAINING SIGNS	HOW I CAN RECOVER
_____	_____
_____	_____
_____	_____
_____	_____
_____	_____
_____	_____
_____	_____
_____	_____
_____	_____

Self-Compassion

I consistently see clients who come in looking for help recovering from narcissistic abuse and are almost abusive to themselves. Almost always, the people who have suffered the abuse of a narcissist are extremely critical of themselves and hold themselves to expectations and standards they would not impose on others.

Self-compassion is giving ourselves the same understanding and love that we often find easy to give to others. It recognizes that we are human and will make mistakes and that these mistakes do not define our worth. Life with a narcissist is fraught with insults, criticism, and other vicious words directed at us. When we hear this long and often enough, we start to believe it to be true. Part of self-compassion is recognizing that those abusive words were lies told to you by a person who was motivated to control you. It is now time to shake away that negative vitriol and learn to be your own biggest fan.

How to Show Yourself Compassion

You may struggle to show yourself compassion because you have not experienced much compassion being shown to you. I would like to offer a simple exercise so you can see that you likely have an abundance of compassion within yourself—the task you have is to start sharing it with yourself.

Please write down an example of something you did that you feel some shame around.

_____

_____

_____

Now take a moment to recall an event from your childhood self that left you feeling ashamed, perhaps from when you were between ages 5 and 10. Write down what you think that child would need to hear so they no longer feel shame for this event.

_____

_____

_____

_____

_____

_____

As we grow and learn—over the course of weeks or the span of decades—we typically walk a path of doing better in life. We learn lessons from our experiences and make adjustments that work well for us. Show compassion to yourself the way you would to the inner child in this exercise as you move forward. Continue to use this exercise, especially if you find yourself ruminating on past mistakes, to develop a habit of self-compassion.

The Child Within

We all carry wounds and joy from the past. Nostalgia from the smell of grandma's lasagna brings us joy. By reliving something we regret, we are holding on to shame that likely stems from early wounds we may have been carrying since before we had the words to even describe exactly how we were hurt. I encourage you to find a quiet place and relax your gaze or close your eyes and seek out that child within you who is feeling shame. Reflect on their feelings. On the following lines or in a notebook, write them a letter. Some suggestions:

- Tell them that they are loved.

- Tell them that as they have grown, they have learned from the mistakes they made as a child.

- Let them know that they are worthy of being loved just because of who they are.

_____

_____

_____

_____

_____

_____

_____

_____

_____

_____

_____

_____

_____

_____

_____

_____

_____

_____

_____

As you write, check in with emotions that touch on childhood wounds and keep comforting that inner child. Also, keep experiencing joyful moments that come up and awaken that inner child.

Forgive Yourself

So many of us falsely believe that we've done things to create the abusive situation we are in, or perhaps that we deserve to be treated poorly. If you have more than one abusive relationship in your past, it is likely because this is the only type of relationship you recognize and that feels familiar. This often stems from early childhood emotional wounds we carry with us into adulthood. It is time to stop blaming yourself and learn to forgive yourself for not knowing better. Please bring to mind a mistake you have made. Write it here:

_____

_____

_____

Now try saying it out loud in a private space where you cannot be heard by others.
    Now write down what you would have done differently if you knew then what you know now.

_____

_____

_____

_____

Now say this out loud. Next, purposefully and powerfully tell yourself, "I forgive myself and I recognize that I did not have the knowledge then to make better choices."
    Repeat this exercise with more than one mistake if that's what you need. This prompt is a step toward releasing yourself from old pain.

Loving-Kindness Meditation

The purpose of this meditation is to nurture compassion and goodwill within yourself. Directing love and kindness toward yourself is the first step in fully giving it to others from a genuinely loving space.

1. Please find a comfortable and quiet place to sit.

2. Close your eyes or soften your gaze and start to notice the rise and fall of your breath.

3. Bring your attention to the confused or shame-filled inner child you connected with previously.

4. Let the love and kindness you have for that child flow forth, and wish that inner child peace, joy, and love for the rest of their life.

5. Now think about those closest to you, and let the love flow forth with wishes of peace and joy attached.

6. Now move to people at work, in your neighborhood, and in other circles and give them the same love and wishes.

7. Practice this often to build your habit of love, kindness, and acceptance so it becomes second nature to you.

Mastering the Skill of Assertiveness

Assertiveness can be confused with aggressiveness, but they are quite different. In a nutshell, being assertive is a more respectful approach. Practicing assertiveness can feel foreign and uncomfortable at first, but it's an essential skill to learn. This exercise dovetails with the practice of noticing physical reactions and trusting that they are guiding us correctly, because it allows us to act on our reactions in a way that protects us.

To practice assertiveness, bring to mind an event in which you found it difficult to assert or stick up for yourself. For example, your children's mother, who has narcissistic traits, keeps asking you to pick up the kids after school even though it's her turn. She uses guilt to manipulate you, despite its inconvenience to you. A way to assertively express yourself in this situation would be to say that you are unable to do so on such short notice. You can offer to revisit the pickup schedule in the future so this does not continue to happen.

Now, thinking of the event you have in mind, write down an assertive statement of how you might speak up for yourself:

Self-Affirmations

Self-affirmations are a great way to practice accepting and loving yourself. Use the examples listed here to start saying kind words to yourself aloud. Visualize your inner child as you do this, and look in the mirror so your present self can benefit, too. Repeat this activity daily so that it really becomes ingrained in you as your go-to way of thinking about yourself.

- I do not have to do anything to earn love; I already deserve it.

- I am safe and loved.

- It's okay to be honest.

- I am worthy of love and kindness just by being me.

- I will protect you no matter what.

- I love you just the way you are.

- I am the most valuable investment I will ever make.

Start Building Your Self-Esteem

To me, an accurate definition of self-esteem is *confidence and belief in your own worth*. To start building self-esteem, use the list on page 56 to start incorporating some of these mindsets and behaviors in your daily life. Return to this list often to check in, and feel free to add your own ideas. Keep track of each time you use one of these mindsets and behaviors to improve your self-esteem.

MINDSETS AND BEHAVIORS	TALLY
Look at a mistake as a learning opportunity.	
Do not compare yourself to others.	
Recognize that there is no "one right way" to do anything.	
Express anger in a creative way.	
Recognize that your problems are not unique.	
Accept your weaknesses and strengths.	
Notice moments of confidence.	

Building Self-Confidence

For this exercise, we will complete a personal SWOT (Strengths, Weaknesses, Opportunities, and Threats) analysis. This will help you identify how these four items affect your confidence, so you can see where your confidence already exists and where it needs work. Imagine a goal you'd like to work toward—for example, to be more assertive. Thinking of this goal, in each quadrant, write traits that you already possess. In the two left quadrants, take pride/satisfaction in the traits/wishes you have identified. In the two right quadrants, note what you would like to improve or eliminate. This exercise can help you see how far you've come and help you recognize that where you want to be is within reach.

STRENGTHS	WEAKNESSES
Example: History of standing up for myself	Example: Fear of consequences if I am assertive
OPPORTUNITIES	THREATS
Example: Be more forthcoming about my needs and having them met	Example: Not being taken seriously because I have not been assertive in a long time

Write Your Story

Another way to build your confidence is to write a story about your life. You can do this on your computer or in a notebook or journal. The narrative can be brief, but make it detailed enough to note areas of success and how you have overcome setbacks. Write as though you are writing about a beloved friend or family member. Take moments to experience any emotions that arise for you, and if they are negative, practice self-love and forgiveness learned in the previous exercises. Sit with any positive feelings for a while and feel the pride and self-love that belongs to you.

By writing your story, you give a gift to yourself in many ways. You are allowing yourself to radically accept who you are and what you have experienced. You are taking pride in getting to where you are now by seeking tools to recover. You are learning to love and accept yourself unconditionally. And you are courageous enough to move away from toxic relationships and learn how to stay away from them in the future.

Get Comfortable Feeling Your Emotions

Learning more about yourself may have stirred up lots of emotions. That is okay. Many of us spend so much time trying to avoid our feelings that we turn to unhealthy habits and dissociate because we don't want to feel what we feel. Emotions are natural and serve many purposes for us, so I encourage you to take these opportunities as they arise, to really feel what you are feeling. If it's uncomfortable but bearable, remind yourself that an emotion only lasts for a very short time, and then just notice the emotion as it passes through you. If it feels unbearable, come back to this exercise when you are feeling more resilient and distract yourself with a calming activity like positive self-affirmations. Ultimately, understanding your emotions removes any control they have over you and helps you feel braver.

REAL-LIFE STORY: ANGELA

Angela is a former client who really struggled with self-esteem and confidence. She avoided feeling her emotions at all costs and would use the logic part of her brain to convince herself that there was no need to feel anything, because if she did, she would lose control. Angela had been severely neglected and emotionally abused. As a child, she had to care for her siblings because her single mother was not prepared to be a parent. As she got older, Angela found herself in toxic relationships. Despite her ability to identify some horrific behavior in her partners, she always found a way to self-blame for small things that happened in the relationships instead of assigning blame where it belonged.

As Angela worked toward healing, she started to allow herself to explore different emotions and sit with the ones she could identify with. Over time, Angela got to know herself in a way she never had before and recognized that a fear of being abandoned left her guarding her emotions and allowing toxic men into her life. As she gained love for herself, she eventually fell in love with and married a man who treats her with respect, and she is now assertive enough to address issues as they come up. She is learning to love herself more and more and maintains boundaries when things do not feel right to her.

Conclusion

Throughout this chapter, you have taken a close look at yourself—that is something to be extremely proud of. It's challenging to sit with and accept the need to change behaviors and traits that do not benefit you. The courage and tenacity you have shown by getting through this chapter are evidence of your strength. As you put the practices from this chapter into your routine, you will find yourself emerging like a phoenix from the ashes. This work is life-changing, and loving and accepting yourself for who you are will lead to creating better boundaries and paying attention to red flags when you come across someone who is not healthy to have in your life.

Next, we'll explore how to create strong boundaries and an environment in which you can thrive and grow. This is how you begin to show others—and yourself—that you respect yourself and will no longer allow toxicity in your relationships.

CHAPTER 5

Establish Clear Boundaries

In this chapter, we'll get to the heart of where change really happens. Establishing boundaries is putting into action everything you have learned about yourself and your needs. The first step to creating boundaries is understanding what boundaries you need. We will then look at how to create both internal and external boundaries for relationships and environment. Any boundary you create is in service of your own well-being.

I often hear clients ask, "What if they ignore my boundary?" The beauty of creating boundaries is that there are consequences when those boundaries are crossed, and you are in control of all of this. The great thing about having boundaries is that they are yours, and no one chooses how you create or respond to them except you.

REAL-LIFE STORY: ALIYAH

One term used often in recovery from narcissistic abuse is "no-contact." This means shutting down any communication with the narcissist and blocking any access they may have to you through social media or any other avenue. My client Aliyah learned through trial and error how important boundaries were with her mother, who kept trying to control Aliyah despite the fact that she had graduated from college and was emerging into adulthood. Aliyah's mother manipulated her into feeling guilty any time she wanted to explore her independence. She would intrude on Aliyah's relationships, even communicating with Aliyah's friends and boyfriend without her knowledge. Her mother also isolated Aliyah from the few family members they had in the United States, leaving her without any support, aside from the friendships her mother was now intruding upon.

Aliyah and her mother lived together until, one day, her mother became physically abusive. Aliyah left and moved in with her boyfriend. Her mother still tried to control her, but as Aliyah became more comfortable with her newfound freedom, she started putting boundaries in place with her mother and would not tolerate disrespectful communication. Her mother could not respect these boundaries, so to keep her own peace, Aliyah initiated no-contact with her mother. This has worked extremely well and has allowed Aliyah time to heal and work on asserting herself in other situations, as she learns to honor her self-worth.

Understanding the Purpose of Boundaries

As mentioned earlier, boundaries are for you, not the other person. This means that you decide what your boundary is, when it has been crossed, and what the consequence will be for the person who crosses it. This is all for you to maintain your self-love, self-respect, and confidence. The people who will cross boundaries are likely those who have played a role in your feeling unworthy. It will be difficult to change the dynamic in those relationships, but entirely worth the effort. Narcissists and other emotionally abusive people don't like losing control or being told that you will no longer tolerate their behavior.

You might be just beginning to learn how to stand up for yourself; if so, this may feel uncomfortable for a little while. I promise, with consistency and follow-through, boundaries are the way to reclaim your rights and identity and teach people appropriate ways to treat you. It is important, as we move through this chapter, that you prepare to embrace the discomfort of practicing the boundary skills you will learn. Eventually, you will see that the boundaries should have been there all along, and what you are doing by enforcing them is basic self-care that can be integral to who you are without guilt. People will push against your boundaries, but remember, this is how you teach them the proper way to treat you moving forward.

What Does It Mean to Have a Boundary?

Boundaries define where one thing ends and another begins. In this case, boundaries help you define what you are comfortable with and what you are not comfortable with. A narcissist only sees themselves and your being in service to them, so there is no beginning or end between the two of you in their point of view.

In this exercise, I challenge you to make a list of behaviors you have tolerated that you wish to no longer tolerate. Recall moments when you felt that knot in your stomach when someone requested something from you and caused you to feel uncomfortable, and write them down in the space provided. We'll use this list as a starting point to create boundaries around specific situations so you can start putting them into practice right away.

_____

_____

_____

_____

_____

_____

Take a Moment to Sit with Your Emotions

Now that you have created the list from the previous exercise, you might be feeling some unpleasant emotions. Take time to notice what you are feeling and identify any emotions you are experiencing. Please label your emotions and write them on page 64, then take inventory of how you are feeling in relation to each one and write that next to what you have labeled. Remember that emotions come and go rather quickly, and these feelings will pass. Labeling and recognizing your emotions will help you know yourself better and what triggers your emotional responses.

Emotion (example: shame):

_____

What I am feeling physically and mentally (example: Like I can't do anything right):

_____

_____

_____

Emotion:

_____

What I am feeling physically and mentally:

_____

_____

_____

Emotion:

_____

What I am feeling physically and mentally:

_____

_____

_____

Engage in Self-Care

The previous two exercises might have felt emotionally challenging. Take time to recharge and rest by stepping away from the book for as long as you need to in order to practice self-care. You can do something as simple as splashing water on your face, or you can call it a wrap and come back to the workbook later or even tomorrow. When you come back, write about how it felt to care for yourself.

_____

_____

_____

_____

_____

Get a Taste of What Strong Boundaries Feel Like

1. Please find a comfortable place to sit with feet planted firmly on the floor.

2. Place your hands on your lap and soften your gaze or close your eyes.

3. Notice the rhythm of your breath and look toward the future.

4. Imagine a conversation with the narcissist in your life that caused you to feel that knot in your stomach.

5. Now watch as you imagine your future self being assertive and telling the narcissist that it is not okay to speak to you that way or that you do not have time for a conversation right now.

6. Notice what you feel in asserting your boundaries. Let that feeling guide you as you put this new behavior into action.

What Are Internal Boundaries?

Many of my clients self-identify as "people pleasers," which means they typically put the needs of others before their own. The following statements are examples of some boundaries that can lead to honoring yourself. They all build a boundary around your own actions. Here are some examples:

- It's not my job to fix others.

- It's okay if others get angry.

- It's okay to say "no."

- It's not my job to take responsibility for others.

- I do not need to anticipate the needs of others.

- It is my job to make ME happy.

- It is not necessary for others to agree with me.

- I have a right to my own feelings, and they are valid.

- I am enough.

Some of these statements may resonate well with you, and I invite you to add them to your repertoire. For this exercise, please write some internal boundaries that match your needs.

_____

_____

_____

_____

_____

What Are External Boundaries?

You may be more familiar with what external boundaries look like, because a violation of these boundaries can seem more obvious. In one of my own relationships with a narcissist (I have had two), my narcissist would not let me have privacy in the bathroom—an obvious violation of my external boundary of privacy. Other external boundaries include:

- I'm allowed time to myself.

- I have freedom to express myself spiritually.

- I can have my own interests.

- I can work at the job of my choice.

- I maintain my own integrity.

- I control who touches me and when.

- I get to choose the volume of my music.

- I can choose to keep my door locked.

As with the previous exercise, please write down some external boundaries that fit your needs.

_____

_____

_____

_____

_____

_____

_____

_____

_____

_____

_____

_____

_____

_____

Maintaining and Enforcing Internal Boundaries

How do we enforce and maintain internal boundaries? This may feel uncomfortable and foreign at first, but it's essential for healing and for understanding and getting back in touch with who you are. So much of our identities are lost when our lives are consumed with the abuse received by a narcissist that we have to build ourselves back up to be whole again. Understanding and respecting our own internal and external boundaries is crucial in the healing and recovery process. Enforcing boundaries consistently is how we maintain them for the long run. And as mentioned earlier, enforcing them means having consequences for those who violate them.

In my earlier example of my narcissist never letting me have privacy in the bathroom, my consequence was leaving the bathroom every time he entered. It was a small consequence, but it worked, because it created a conditioned response on his part that he learned not to expect my attention in this room.

For this exercise, please choose one or two internal boundaries you identified for yourself in the previous exercise, and write consequences to those boundary violations that will help you enforce the boundaries.

_____

_____

_____

_____

_____

_____

Maintaining and Enforcing External Boundaries

This is going to look different than maintaining internal boundaries, because this work is about letting others know what you will be doing for yourself and that could mean taking privileges (which they did not earn and do not deserve) away from them. This will reduce the power they have over you, and they're likely to challenge you as you enforce your boundaries.

It will take patience and perseverance on your part, and it will be worth it. You may feel like you're talking to a small child when you repeatedly enforce your boundaries until the narcissist sees that you are consistent and serious. As with the previous exercise, please choose one or two external boundaries you have identified for yourself, and note consequences to those boundary violations that will help you enforce them.

_____

_____

_____

_____

_____

It's Okay to Put Your Needs First

Some readers will think they are being selfish if they put their needs before the needs of others. Many of us worry about disappointing others and will often sacrifice ourselves to avoid doing so. One of my favorite analogies for giving yourself permission to put your needs first is the way a flight attendant tells you to place the oxygen mask over your own nose and mouth before helping others who may need your assistance. Please start thinking about this as you move through the next few days and weeks, and take opportunities to check in with what you need and say "yes" to yourself. Then write how you did this.

_____

_____

_____

_____

_____

_____

_____

_____

_____

Expand Your Boundaries to Everyday Situations

It's helpful to recognize how important boundaries are in all aspects of life. Boundaries can be practiced in many different situations, such as with your children, in your place of employment, with non-narcissistic friends and relatives, etc. In this exercise, I challenge you to recall examples where something was asked of you that you said "yes" to but wished you had said "no." This will help you recognize more fully who you are and what matters to you. After you have identified some examples from your history, write them down—then rewrite the ending. Write the ending that you wish had happened. This will help you get used to feeling okay with saying "no" and knowing how to do it.

_____

_____

_____

_____

_____

_____

_____

_____

Challenge Yourself to Say "No"

I encourage you to stand in front of the mirror and practice saying the word "no." This may sound silly, but it's a powerful word to get used to saying. The more you repeat the word "no," the more natural it will feel to say and hear coming from your own voice. Give it a try and practice it often until it's second nature to you.

Advocating for Yourself

Boundaries are part of self-care and healing; so is advocating for yourself. Many people who find themselves in a relationship with a narcissist have experienced trauma and may be reluctant to ask for help because there was nobody they could trust to ask for help in the past. Self-advocacy, or taking action for your own needs and wishes, is a way for your voice to be heard and to remind yourself that you matter.

Try this exercise to think of how you can put it into action. First, write down an area of your life or type of situation in which you would like to practice self-advocacy:

Example: I want to go back to school.

_____

_____

_____

Now write down some steps you can take to do this:

Example: I will find three potential schools and make inquiries.

_____

_____

_____

_____

For the next part of the exercise, think of how you will advocate for yourself when you are questioned or put on the spot about your decision or action.

I.   Say why it is important.

Example: I want to learn a trade or gain knowledge for myself.

_____

_____

_____

_____

2. Describe your intention and plan.

Example: I will be going to school on Tuesday and Thursday evenings to work toward my degree and will need you to care for the children while I am gone.

_____

_____

_____

_____

3. Assert yourself firmly and calmly.

Example: This is something I have wanted to do for a long time, and I am choosing to take time to achieve this goal now.

_____

_____

_____

4. Be persistent in stating your intention or plan.

Example: I am going back to school. If you will not care for the children while I am in class, my sister will.

_____

_____

_____

Practice this exercise with different types of scenarios, so you can learn how to use it in varying situations.

The Empath

Many people are noticing their empathic tendencies and are getting more in touch and comfortable with them. There is a lot of talk out there about how those who consider themselves highly sensitive and empathic became that way. Some believe that highly sensitive and empathic people learn to be that way through their own trauma. After experiencing abuse and/or neglect, they develop a deep understanding of what that feels like and notice it easily in others. Some believe that people are born with these characteristics. Either way, there are sensitive people who feel deep empathy, and you might identify as being one of those people.

This can feel like a blessing and a curse. It may also play a role in our difficulty in removing ourselves from a relationship with a narcissist. We see the world from an empathic point of view and cannot put ourselves in the shoes of someone who victimizes others. When we see narcissistic behaviors, we try to make sense of their behavior through our own lens of empathy, and it makes no sense. We then attribute the behavior as being a one-off or abnormality, but eventually, we see that it is the opposite. The behavior that we've made excuses for is actually the heart of who the narcissist is. Our empathic and sensitive ways have made us ignore what later seems obvious.

Are You an Empath?

There are lots of resources to help you identify whether or not you are an empath, but I believe you know yourself better than any Internet quiz knows you. Some typical characteristics of self-described empaths include: feeling the pain of others, intuitiveness, sensitivity, lacking aggression, and finding it difficult to say "no." If any of these characteristics resonate with you, please note which ones, and then write down how they have helped you and how they have gotten in your way. As you continue to learn more about yourself, you'll learn how to better protect yourself.

PROS TO BEING AN EMPATH

CONS TO BEING AN EMPATH

_____

_____

_____

_____

_____

_____

_____

_____

_____

_____

What Do I Do Now?

As you understand more about yourself and your sensitivity and empathy, consider how they have played a role in where you are now and how you will move forward. Understanding your level of empathy can help you protect yourself from situations that can hurt you emotionally. Many people who consider themselves to be empaths have a hard time watching or being around situations that are even remotely painful. The next time you are with others, or even if you are watching TV or a movie, pay attention to the content that brings emotion to you. Notice how you feel and think about what might make you feel better. Then write about it here.

_____

_____

_____

_____

_____

_____

_____

_____

_____

Manage Your Sensitivity

We know that self-care and boundaries are important, and the process of healing from an abusive relationship can be physically and emotionally exhausting. In this exercise, please take inventory of the demands you routinely face, then make note of how you can reduce what overwhelms you the most in your routine—for example, cooking dinner. The decision-making alone can feel tremendous when you are overwhelmed. An example of reducing the pressure of this demand might be to meal prep for the week or ask someone else to cook or plan dinner a few days of the week. What can you do to reduce the feeling of being overwhelmed?

DEMANDS

TOOLS TO REDUCE FEELING OVERWHELMED

_____ → _____

_____ → _____

_____ → _____

_____ → _____

_____ → _____

REAL-LIFE STORY: ELIJAH

Elijah struggled his entire adult life with boundaries with his father. Elijah was treated as a scapegoat in his family of origin and, even into adulthood, his father tried to orchestrate the dynamics between Elijah and his sister, who was considered the golden child. The sister could do no wrong, while Elijah was blamed for nearly everything.

After spending some time in therapy and working hard on boundaries and self-love, Elijah set strict boundaries with his father and was quite specific about what he would and would not tolerate from him. As his father continued to disrespect Elijah's boundaries, Elijah began to tighten them up and cautioned his father that if his behavior did not change, Elijah would go no-contact. Elijah's father would not listen and, after going no-contact, his father showed up at Elijah's place of employment to try to talk to him. Elijah stood his ground and did not indulge his father.

He later advocated for himself by writing a letter to his father to enforce another consequence and let his father know he would be changing his phone number and, after a move that he and his partner had already planned, would not be providing his parents with his new address. Elijah was clear with his father about his boundaries and established increasingly firm consequences as his father continued to violate them. Elijah is still no-contact with his father, and he is at peace with that and living his best life.

Conclusion

My hope is that you have gained some tools and understanding of who you are at your core and how to better respect yourself. Boundaries are the fundamental skill for recovering from a narcissistic relationship and have the added bonus of helping you know and love yourself better. Boundaries can and should be practiced in all areas of life, as we will undoubtedly encounter rude, inconsiderate, and narcissistic people anywhere we go.

Having the skill to self-advocate and decide what is and is not tolerable is a way to create healthy relationships and a positive environment for your future self. In the next chapter, we will focus on creating and maintaining healthy relationships and letting go of unhealthy ways of thinking that have led to toxic relationships in the past.

PART THREE

Healing Takes Time

In the final section of this workbook, we will look at how to move forward with the skills you are learning and with patience. There is an instinct to want to rush the healing process. Of course you want to feel better and get on with your new life, but it took a long time to understand and start to protect yourself from the abuse, and it will take time to heal. Patience is required to incorporate self-love, self-esteem, and a sense of identity and to develop boundaries. Change happens slowly, so we must notice the differences as they are happening. Small goals will allow you to see the wins as they happen and keep you motivated.

You've got this!

CHAPTER 6

Nurture Healthy Relationships

It is shocking how easy it is to slip back into old habits, especially when one has been in a relationship with a narcissist for any length of time. Their behavior is familiar and starts to feel "normal." The goal of this chapter is to help you recognize this normalization of narcissistic abuse and to be mindful of not letting it happen. This chapter will also provide you with the skills to avoid toxic relationships and nurture healthy ones. We'll discuss the importance of a strong support network to help you stay on track. We'll also examine how odd it may feel to have supportive people around you. Before you know it, healthy, honest, and supportive people will be the type that is normal to you instead of chaotic, toxic people who bring upheaval into your life.

There is continually more understanding of narcissistic abuse, and support groups are available through a quick Internet search. I encourage you to seek support in ways that are most comfortable—maybe even consider starting a support group of your own.

REAL-LIFE STORY: BRIANNA AND DERRICK (PART I)

Brianna and Derrick married young, and both came from dysfunctional families. They thought they were soul mates, but Derrick was angry to his core and could not express his emotions without being violent. They divorced after six years but had to stay in contact because of their two children. Over time, Brianna saw Derrick getting more manipulative and emotionally abusive to her, to their children, and then to his new wife and their children. She realized that she had met Derrick in the early part of the development of his narcissistic personality disorder and watched it get worse over the years.

Cognitive dissonance (we'll explore this concept more on page 83) and the desperate need to feel loved kept Brianna from seeing Derrick as he was. When he started manipulating their children, she realized what he had become. She started her healing process by first protecting her children from the pain she experienced, then realized that this protection had to happen in all areas of her life. She started putting strong boundaries in all relationships that were unhealthy for her and her children and sought out healthy relationships. She learned to love herself and modeled this behavior for her children.

Your Moment of Realization

Please take a moment to reflect on your instant of realization: that moment when you recognized the narcissist for who they truly are. It might be when you picked up this book or it might have happened years ago, or anywhere in between. I genuinely believe when that moment hits, or when it is an "aha" moment, that's when you start thinking of what is best for you. Take note of what that "aha" moment was for you, write about it here, and refer to it often.

_____

_____

_____

_____

_____

_____

What Is Cognitive Dissonance?

There is no term that better describes how being with a narcissist feels than "cognitive dissonance." With cognitive dissonance, we filter out information that is obviously true so we can hold on to a belief that serves us. This might be justifying a narcissist's rages by convincing yourself that they are not as bad as they seem. You might tell yourself that they are not always like this, because remember that time you went to the amusement park and had so much fun? Without the cognitive dissonance, you can probably count on one hand how many good days there were in your relationship, which pales in comparison to the bad days.

It is a true wake-up call when cognitive dissonance loses its effectiveness and you really see things for what they are. It might sound scary, but when you get to this point, it is liberating. You get to start making decisions based on what actually is instead of what could be "if only."

Check In with Cognitive Dissonance

Understanding cognitive dissonance is such a huge part of healing. Reflect on the relationship you had with a narcissist and see if you can recognize times when you may have had cognitive dissonance. One of the best ways to recognize it is remembering when you have gone along with something when something inside was telling you to say "no." If you find yourself questioning your own response to something, it is a good time to look deeper to find out what's happening. Write about your experience here.

_____

_____

_____

_____

_____

Healthy or Not Healthy?

Read the following statements, then circle which ones you feel are acceptable in a healthy relationship.

- To say "no" without feeling guilty

- To change my mind without a reason

- To make mistakes

- To express thoughts and ideas

- To ask questions

- To express feelings even if they feel negative

- To say "I don't know"

- To ask for help

- To take a minute to think before acting on something

- To expect respect all the time

- To feel good about myself

- To assert a personal right

You might have recognized that all these statements are true in a healthy relationship. Whether you circled or did not circle any of the items above, it is worth reflecting on your reasoning. If there are some statements that you did not circle, please take some time to question why the statement did not align with what you think of as healthy in a relationship, and challenge yourself to see it differently.

A Quick Mantra

Repeating positive statements to yourself helps you believe them and internalize them. Each morning before you get out of bed, and each night before your head hits the pillow, say the following statements aloud:

- I will set realistic expectations for myself.

- I will let go of things I cannot change.

- I will love myself as I am.

Recognizing Cognitive Dissonance

How do you know, in the moment, if you are experiencing cognitive dissonance? It takes some time to understand and some practice to recognize it. However, once you can identify it and catch the signals when something seems "off," you've got helpful tools with which you can see things clearly. Take the quiz below and see if you are prone to cognitive dissonance. Check off the statements that apply to you:

☐ I feel conflicted without really understanding why.

☐ I feel confused after a conversation with the narcissist.

☐ I sometimes feel that pit in my stomach after I have agreed to something.

☐ I make excuses or rationalize their behavior.

☐ I have lied to myself about things not being "that bad."

☐ I have convinced myself that their bad behavior is forgivable because the good behavior is the "real" person.

☐ I have done things that are in conflict with my belief system.

Each of these statements is an example of cognitive dissonance. If you have checked more than three items, it is likely that you are experiencing significant cognitive dissonance. Please remember that this is common in abusive relationships. Also remember that it is not a life sentence, and part of what you are learning on your path to recovery is about getting rid of these unhealthy ways of thinking.

Correcting Cognitive Dissonance

There is a cartoon that shows two booths: One has a sign that says UNPLEASANT TRUTHS and the other says COMFORTING LIES. Guess which one people in the cartoon are lined up to hear? The "comforting lies" line is quite long while there is no one in line for the "unpleasant truths" line. So how do we correct this? Much of what you have learned in this workbook has already prepared you to face this way of thinking, but I would like to offer some tools to help you correct cognitive dissonance so you can create and maintain healthy relationships. We'll do this by exploring each of the statements in the previous exercise.

Feeling conflicted without really understanding why.

Take as much time as you need to sit with this discomfort and sort it out. It's okay to change your mind about something if you decide that it does not work for you.

Having confusion after a conversation with your narcissist.

Ask for clarification and stick to the facts. They will try to manipulate you; if that starts, walk away, then revisit the issue later.

Feeling that pit in your stomach after you have agreed to something.

That pit in your stomach is your red flag warning—don't ignore it! Again, remember that you can change your mind and say "no" whenever you need to or want to.

Making excuses or rationalizing someone else's behavior.

This is common in abusive relationships. If you find yourself doing this, take a step back in your thinking and apply responsibility where it belongs. This helps you accept the uncomfortable truths.

Lying to yourself about things not being that bad.

This is another opportunity to stand in the "uncomfortable truths" line. Facing the discomfort helps us recognize what is really happening and allows us to choose whether or not we want to be a part of it. The same is true for the statement in which you convince yourself that the bad behavior is acceptable because the good behavior is the "real" person. Look at the uncomfortable truth.

You do things that conflict with your belief system.

As you regain your true self and pay attention to your internal reaction to things, you will be able to maintain commitment to your belief system and no longer stray from it.

Check In on Your Healthy Relationships

Over the next few days or so, think about cognitive dissonance and see if and how it is playing a role in any other relationships. Take notice if there are some relationships in which this happens more and some in which it happens less. Keep track of which people in your life fit into each category and apply what you have learned. You will likely find that you start placing boundaries on some other relationships as you go through this process.

I have found that cognitive dissonance occurs in these relationships:

_____

_____

_____

_____

I have found that these relationships are true and authentic:

_____

_____

_____

_____

Are You People Pleasing?

Whether we learned it early on or when we met our first narcissist, most of us have learned to people please to gain approval and acceptance and keep the peace. The act of people pleasing, to me, is like being in survival mode. We give up what's important to us in order to keep someone else content because we just want to be able to manage, which gives us no room to thrive. There is no shame in this behavior, but it is something we can unlearn.

Some people-pleasing tendencies will go away as you practice loving and accepting yourself, and some of it will take work to change. Nurturing healthy relationships starts with nurturing your relationship with yourself. This will, on its own, lead to a reduction in people pleasing. We will also look at ways to recognize this behavior and stop it proactively.

What Are Signs of People Pleasing?

The number-one question I want to ask you about people pleasing is: *How afraid of the fallout are you if you say "no"?* Saying "no" is a boundary, but the fear of their reaction can feel over-whelming to us, and we often cannot move past that and just keep the peace by saying "yes." Please answer the questions below to get an idea of where you are with people pleasing.

1.	Are you afraid of the negative consequences if you say "no" to someone?	Yes	No
2.	Do you take the blame even it is not your fault?	Yes	No
3.	Do you give and give but do not often receive? (This can be emotionally or tangibly.)	Yes	No
4.	Do you feel lonely despite having others around you?	Yes	No
5.	Are you hiding your real self from others?	Yes	No
6.	Do you *need* people to like you?	Yes	No

What Does People Pleasing Mean to You?

Please look at your answers in the previous exercise and reflect on them, especially your answer to the first question. I believe that all the behaviors in questions 2 through 6 ultimately come back to question 1: What are the consequences? An important thing to recognize and remember is that the consequences are probably not nearly as bad as you might be afraid they are. Take some time to reflect on this and write down your thoughts in the space that follows. What do you think is the worst-case scenario, and what is most likely to happen? You can come back to this anytime you need a reminder on this subject.

_____

_____

_____

_____

_____

_____

_____

_____

_____

_____

Understanding Guilt and Shame So You Can Heal

Guilt and shame are stumbling blocks I see with many of my clients. They worry that any self-nurturing and self-care means that they, themselves, are narcissistic. If you feel this way, please stop and recognize the first big difference between you and the narcissist in your life: You have empathy, and they likely have little or none. Like many things in a relationship with a narcissist, understanding what you are feeling guilt or shame around can feel foggy and hard to name. Let us start this exercise by naming what we are feeling and why.

When you feel shame, you may slump your shoulders, have a weary expression on your face, or put your face in your hands as if you are hiding. Emotionally, you may feel a sense of embarrassment or that you are flawed. Note here what shame looks and feels like to you:

_____

_____

_____

_____

When you feel guilt, you may look like you're hiding by keeping your head down and not making eye contact. Emotionally, it can feel like you are not good enough and not worthy. Write about how you look and feel when you experience guilt:

_____

_____

_____

_____

Forgiving Yourself

An important piece of letting go of guilt and shame is to radically accept that something happened in the past that you regret and cannot change. This means not getting lost in thinking about "If only I had done this or that differently" or "I'm a bad person." That type of thinking keeps us from letting go of the past and clinging to old habits.

Often when we have done things that we felt guilt or shame around, we did them when we did not know better. As Maya Angelou once said, "When you know better, you do better." This is a nice sentence to repeat to yourself when you are working toward forgiveness. If your 17-year-old self did something that your 37-year-old self is still feeling guilty about, it's time to forgive that 17-year-old and let them know that the grown-up version of you knows better now.

In this exercise, I would like you to write down at least one incident that you have felt guilt over and one incident that you have felt shame about. Then I want you to forgive yourself for those incidents by talking to yourself like you would if you were speaking with a friend, child, or other loved one.

I have felt guilt over:

_____

_____

_____

_____

Forgiveness statement:

_____

_____

_____

_____

I have felt shame over:

_____

_____

Forgiveness statement:

_____

_____

_____

_____

Recognizing Problematic Patterns

Let's talk about recognizing problematic patterns. I can confess that this was a big shift for me that I am still working on. Knowing and accepting my problematic patterns helped me be closer to the people I love, because I am learning to do better at taking feedback when I have done something that does not sit right with someone else.

After many years in two different narcissistic relationships, I learned to be very defensive and sensitive to criticism. This made it difficult for me to tolerate the guilt and shame I felt if I had inadvertently hurt someone. My instinct has been to run away or shut down, which only makes things worse. I also process things slowly, and I try to let my loved ones know this so they don't think I'm avoiding their concerns. To address and change problematic patterns, we need to recognize what they are without feeling ashamed or guilty. Again, we need to just accept that we are human and we make mistakes.

For this exercise, please note any patterns in your own behavior that you would like to change. Be kind to yourself as you do this exercise and remember we are all students of life, learning as we go.

Example Problematic Pattern: I notice that when someone implies that I did something wrong, I run away or shut down. I also process things slowly so I don't have a quick response ready.

Problematic pattern 1:

_____

_____

_____

_____

Problematic pattern 2:

_____

_____

_____

_____

Changing Problematic Patterns

Please take the first problematic pattern you wrote down from the previous exercise and look at it from a different point of view. For example: "My problematic pattern is feeling like a complete failure when someone implies that I did something wrong. I get defensive and feel shameful and guilty, then I shut down. I can take a moment to step back and see my behavior from the other person's point of view and take accountability for my mistakes and get comfortable with how vulnerable I feel knowing that I let someone down. As I recognize this pattern, I can start to be more proactive by shutting down this response sequence before it starts, or at least minimizing it by simply communicating in a healthy way."

In the space provided, write about how you can look at your problematic patterns from a different point of view.

Problematic pattern 1:

_____

_____

_____

_____

Problematic pattern 2:

_____

_____

_____

_____

How Are You Spending Your Time?

For this prompt, please do some reflection on who is in your life and where your attention is. Are you spending time with people or a person who lifts you up, who makes you feel happy to be around and leaves you feeling content and maybe even refreshed after spending time together? Are you watching crime shows or violent movies? Are you spending too much time on social media comparing yourself to others? Sit with these questions and notice what brings you joy when it comes to socialization, support, and community, as well as what feels heavy or draining and can be left behind.

I get joy from:

_____

_____

_____

_____

I feel drained by:

_____

_____

_____

_____

Nurturing in Relationships

Let's define some tools you can use to nurture a relationship outside the one you have with yourself. How can you start a relationship on the right track and keep it there? Unfortunately, I do not think many of us are taught how to do this, and we find ourselves muddling around learning from trial and error to figure out what works and what doesn't.

In this exercise, please note how you can put some of the following examples of positive relationships into action. I encourage you to write some ideas of your own and brainstorm how to start incorporating them into your relationships.

Communicate openly.

How can you improve your communication with those you are, or want to be, close with? *Example: I will allow myself to be more open with my daughter in our conversations.*

_____

_____

_____

_____

Be intentional about making time for that person.

Time is one of the most valuable gifts we can give to another; it lets them know they are important to us. How can you set aside time to be with someone?

_____

_____

_____

_____

Tell them how much they mean to you.

Be vulnerable in sharing how much you appreciate that person being a part of your life. Practice what you can say to express this. Write some ideas in the space below.

_____

_____

_____

_____

_____

Clear up any misunderstandings quickly, openly, and honestly.

Write an example of what you might say when you feel as though something has been misconstrued or misunderstood.

_____

_____

_____

_____

_____

Write down your own ideas for nurturing relationships.

_____

_____

_____

_____

_____

REAL-LIFE STORY: LUCY AND JADA

After years with a partner who was a covert narcissist, Lucy decided she was ready to start dating again. She was leery of getting close to anyone, so she kept things casual and held extremely strong boundaries to protect herself from falling into another toxic relationship. She was not finding any strong connections and considered giving up looking for a romantic partner; she gave it one last try and met Jada.

Jada was unique, didn't play games, and was up front with Lucy from the start. Lucy was not used to a partner who was comfortable with their feelings, affectionate without expectations, and generous with compliments and positive statements. When they had disagreements, Lucy did catastrophize, but Jada was right there ready to talk through the conflict instead of running away from the whole relationship. Jada taught Lucy to take a moment before she let the urge to run away overcome her so she could recognize that there was no catastrophe.

Eventually, Lucy learned that if she took a few seconds after she had been emotionally triggered, she could calm herself and talk to Jada about what was happening. Lucy has learned to nurture her relationship with Jada by intentionally connecting with her at certain times to keep communication, affection, and connectedness thriving in their relationship. Now Lucy understands that not every relationship has to feel chaotic and scary. She is content and stable with a partner who adores her and whom she adores as well.

Conclusion

In this chapter, we explored ways to create and maintain healthy relationships, starting by creating a healthy relationship with ourselves and knowing our own vulnerabilities. When you create awareness of yourself and how you are perceived by others, you can adjust things that aren't working and embrace things that are. It is difficult, but taking an honest look at yourself for all that is good and that which you would like to change helps you see what's healthy in others.

Please take joy in your ability to look inward at your behaviors, because that required a good deal of bravery on your part. The result is the gift of knowing how to have healthy connections with others in your life and being on the path to living life as your true, core self. Living in an authentic way is one of the most liberating feelings you might ever have and it is glorious to love, accept, and forgive yourself every day of your life.

CHAPTER 7

Self-Care Comes First

In this final chapter, we'll bring together everything you have learned so you can continue to recover and keep giving love and respect to yourself. Your practice must continue so you can maintain loving and respectful relationships with others. Healing and recovery take time and effort, and you might find yourself having a day here and there where you feel like you are back to square one. I can assure you that you are not, especially if you continue to do the work you started in this book. It is normal to have occasional slips back into old behaviors, but the difference is that now you recognize it and can adjust instead of letting it be a way of life for you.

REAL-LIFE STORY: BRIANNA AFTER DERRICK (PART 2)

After six years together, Brianna left the relationship after seeing how Derrick's selfish and destructive behavior affected their children. It wasn't easy; in fact, Brianna was convinced she was leaving the love of her life and believed it when Derrick told her that no one else would ever love her, but she knew she needed to protect her children. She was brokenhearted and secretly wished she could reunite with Derrick someday after the children were grown, because it would be just her and she felt it didn't matter how he treated her. It was as if she were under a spell and the only thing that made her see reality was her children. Brianna could see how damaging he was to them.

Thankfully, through that awareness, using resources similar to this book, and therapy, Brianna started to believe that she deserved better, too. She realized that Derrick had been gaslighting her and taking away bits and pieces of who she was at her core, and she realized she needed to heal and protect herself as well.

Once away from Derrick, Brianna began creating new friendships and was able to learn to trust people again. She paid close attention to her intuition and has learned to trust it. She also began to speak more nicely to herself, which led to healing other parts of her that had been wounded. The best thing she did for herself was to create boundaries; to this day, if she speaks to Derrick, she has to keep her boundaries strong because while she has changed and grown, he has not.

Reflection and Review

Please use the space provided to reflect on the areas that you have put into practice using the information and activities from this book. Do you still need to work on these areas? Are you in the process, do you have more research to do, etc.? If so, please check the Resources section (page 126) for additional information regarding narcissistic abuse.

Are there any aspects of narcissism you want to learn more about? (The Resources on page 126 may be a good starting point for this.)

_____

_____

_____

_____

Do you know the difference between a covert and an overt narcissist? Where does the narcissist(s) in your life fall on the spectrum?

_____

_____

_____

_____

_____

_____

Have you acknowledged and accepted what you have experienced? If not, how can you move toward this?

_____

_____

_____

_____

_____

_____

Are you comfortable putting self-love, self-compassion, and self-acceptance in practice? If not, reflect on what is stopping you (then return to chapter 4 to get some inspiration).

_____

_____

_____

_____

_____

_____

Have you been able to start recognizing where boundaries are needed and how and when to reinforce them?

_____

_____

_____

_____

_____

Are there unhealthy relationships in your life that you would like to improve or move on from? Do you have ideas of how to nurture healthy new relationships as they start?

_____

_____

_____

_____

_____

Take Pride in How Far You've Come

1. Please find a quiet place to sit with your feet planted firmly on the floor or ground while you notice the surface beneath you. Sit with your back straight and relax your shoulders.

2. Reflect on where you've been, what has happened, and the progress you've made to get to this place in your life.

3. Take a minute to scan your body to notice any areas of tension as you think about this topic and calm the tension (a small stretch, loosening the muscle tension).

4. Now just sit for a minute with pride in the fact that you have taken time to understand what you have been through and how far you have come.

What Are Your Values?

So much of our identity can be wrapped up in people pleasing and keeping the peace with the narcissist in our lives that we no longer know what we want or who we really are. Now is the time to embrace who you are at your core, and perhaps who you left behind as the narcissist in your life started tearing you down. A good place to start your future is thinking about what you value. I've listed a few values here that often resonate with people. Please write a bit about why each value resonates with you. Add any values of your own that might not be on this list and why they are important values to you.

Peace:

_____

_____

Love:

_____

_____

Career:

_____

_____

Family:

_____

_____

Education:

_____

_____

Earth preservation:

_____

_____

Caring for pets:

_____

_____

Exploration/travel:

_____

_____

Religion/spirituality:

_____

_____

Status:

_____

_____

Security:

_____

_____

Other values:

_____

_____

_____

_____

_____

_____

Knowing Your Core Self

At some point in a relationship with a narcissist, we lose touch with our core selves. We become so wrapped up in keeping the peace, trying to understand what is going on, and being insulted, belittled, and lied to, that we get stuck in survival mode. There is little to no room for exploring interests or even time for ourselves. We become blended with the narcissist so we can avoid any negativity from them as much as possible.

One client describes this core self as a tiny little nugget, deep within her, that still exists after many years with a narcissistic husband. Maybe we all have that tiny little nugget, or maybe an even bigger piece, of the person we were before our entanglement with the narcissist, within us. Either way, we must recognize that part of us and use that part as an anchor to help us move forward.

Recognizing the things in life that matter to us is an essential place to start in rebuilding our identity, which has likely been at least partially lost through our experience with the narcissist. Knowing what we value helps reinforce our boundaries, which, as we now know, are the foundation of recovery from narcissistic abuse.

Manifest Your Values

Please go back to your values list (page 103) and pick one or two that you would like to start focusing on. Sit with each value you have chosen and imagine your future self, perhaps a year from now, living true to that value. What does that feel like in your body when you see your future self living in line with what feels authentic? Notice where you feel that in your body, and when it arises, use that feeling as a guide to let you know you are moving in your desired direction. Also, notice if you feel pride, love, or some other positive emotion in your future self. That positive feeling is great motivation to stay on target with what you want. If you start to feel discouraged in the future, come back to this practice and remind yourself how it will feel to live authentically.

Putting Your Values into Action

Look back to the values you identified on page 103 and consider how you can align them with your day-to-day life. For example, if you are interested in keeping the environment clean, how can you make changes in your daily life to align yourself with that value? Do you recycle or volunteer with beach, park, or trail cleanups? Do you choose recyclable or compostable packaging when buying products? If peace is a value, what are you doing to bring peace into your own life? Do you carve out alone time? Do you avoid watching too many news stories or violent movies? These are suggestions for how we can convert ideas into action and live truly with what we value. When you put these ideas into practice, they become part of who you are and help you reclaim your identity, hopefully better than ever.

Choose three of your most important values and brainstorm ways to put them into practice in your everyday life.

Value 1:

_____

_____

_____

Value 2:

_____

_____

_____

Value 3:

_____

_____

_____

How Do You Practice Self-Care?

Let us start by taking inventory of what you might already be doing for self-care. Even small efforts count, so make sure you consider everything from making sure you are getting enough sleep to taking a vacation, if possible. It all counts, and it is important to your overall well-being.

Remember that self-care does not mean you are being selfish. Education is self-care, grocery shopping is self-care, maintaining employment is self-care—and there are many other forms that do not equate to indulgences.

Write about the ways you already practice self-care:

_____

_____

_____

_____

_____

_____

_____

_____

Simple Self-Care Ideas

Now let's explore some new suggestions for self-care rituals that you can easily add to your daily routine. Getting into these habits will likely make you realize just how important each of them is and will lead to your using them when you are feeling "off." As we do self-care rituals more regularly, we gain more insight into what keeps us feeling balanced and healthy, which leads to positive self-esteem. Here are some ideas:

- Give yourself a hug. This puts you in touch with your body and helps you feel grounded.

- Take a few breaths with a 5-second inhale and an 8-second exhale. The longer exhale stimulates your parasympathetic nervous system (the part of the nervous system that returns the body to rest after a stressful situation) and helps you feel calm.

- Disconnect from social media or electronics for an hour.

- Watch the sunset.

- Go for a walk.

- Go to a dog park and watch (and pet) the friendly dogs.

The list can be endless, so think of some small self-care activities that sound appealing to you and add them here.

_____

_____

_____

_____

Recognizing When You Need Self-Care

Admittedly, the title above is misleading—you *always* need to care for yourself; however, until it gets to be routine, you need to find ways to recognize when you need attending to. There may be several signs that you need self-care that you might have gotten used to ignoring or putting off to a time that is more convenient. Failing to engage in self-care can leave us overwhelmed, vulnerable, and easily triggered. Please take a few minutes to write down what happens to you when you're not engaging in sufficient (or any) self-care.

_____

_____

_____

_____

_____

_____

Self-Esteem

The natural step following the incorporation of self-care into your life is increasing self-esteem. You cannot have healthy self-esteem if you don't care for, and honor, yourself. It is vitally important to attend to your self-esteem and build it like you would a muscle, to keep it in good shape. Being in an abusive relationship is a self-esteem killer, but in the particularly insidious and mentally cruel type of abusive relationship with a narcissist, it is almost as though crushing your self-esteem was their main target.

So many successful, smart, creative, and educated people have come to therapy with destroyed self-esteem. No matter their accomplishments or talents, their narcissist has cut them to core and they lose most or all the positive feelings they have for themselves. The narcissist has demanded all your time and attention, leaving very little for yourself. You no longer have the luxury of downtime to recharge because the narcissist has expected you to be there for them. They seem to use an emotional chisel to chip away at you and you forget to value yourself. Now that you are practicing self-love and self-care, we will spend time talking about and learning skills to increase self-esteem.

Where Is Your Self-Esteem Currently?

Please take some time to notice changes in your self-esteem since you have been in a relationship with a narcissist. Was it better prior to your relationship, and if so, how? Did you have confidence? How is that different now? Do you feel less capable of doing things you once did? Are there areas where your self-esteem is strong, despite the emotional abuse you have endured? Are you getting your power back? Write about your self-esteem here, especially where you are now.

_____

_____

_____

_____

_____

Self-Esteem Check-Up

Please circle the statements below that are true to how you feel about yourself. Allow yourself to be vulnerable in your answers so you can really get to the core of how you are feeling. This is another area where vulnerability, honesty, and acceptance will help you become your healthiest self.

- I accept myself as I am with no exceptions.

- I can accept feedback or criticism without feeling unworthy.

- I deserve love and respect.

- I have worth just because I am me.

- I am resilient.

- I am capable.

- I am grateful.

- I believe in myself.

- I am honest.

- I am fair.

- I have courage.

- I have integrity.

- I am responsible for my own actions.

- I like the essence of who I am.

Please list any other characteristics of self-esteem that you possess. If you circled a few, take pride in that! If you do not feel like you circled enough, know that this is something you have the power to improve by building your self-esteem and reflecting on your values.

- _____

- _____

- _____

- _____

What Are You Saying to Yourself?

The first step to better self-esteem is positive self-talk, because if we have low self-esteem, we might be feeding that negative monster with our own disparaging words. You spend the most time with yourself, so it is fundamentally important that you are nice to you! Following are some topics around which you can reframe negative self-talk into positive self-talk. We'll start with a couple of examples, then please fill in your own responses.

- Negative self-talk 1: "Melissa has lost a lot of weight and I am still overweight. I wish I could be more disciplined like her."

- Reframe 1: "I admire Melissa's determination and realize that I am on my own weight loss journey at my own pace and comfort level."

- Negative self-talk 2: "I did miserably at that job interview, and I am sure they thought I was stupid."

- Reframe 2: "I did not do as well as I would have liked at that job interview, and I see where I could have been stronger and will work on that for the next one."

Now please write some negative self-talk you currently engage in and a reframe that is more kind and helpful.

Negative self-talk:

_____

_____

_____

Reframe:

_____

_____

_____

Negative self-talk:

_____

_____

_____

Reframe:

_____

_____

_____

Negative self-talk:

_____

_____

_____

Reframe:

_____

_____

_____

Do you notice how the kind reframes feel more uplifting and even helpful? If this area is an issue, I hope you'll keep working on this daily.

Asserting Yourself

With low self-esteem, it's easy to let people walk all over you and accept unkind treatment from others. This is a dreadful way to live and you deserve much better. Remember not to confuse assertion with aggression—they are distinctly different, and assertiveness will have much better results than aggression. After each of the items you list on page 113, write a response that is assertive and self-protective so you can get a feel for what it is like to speak up for yourself. Start to put this into practice in life as well, to cement the fact that you matter and deserve to be treated respectfully.

Example: Chen, I need you to work overtime because everyone else has said "no."

Assertive response: I've mentioned that I have no childcare on Tuesdays and Thursdays and will not be able to stay late on these days. Please consider someone else.

Please note some of your own instances of being taken advantage of when you would have preferred to be assertive, and note what you would have liked to say at the time.

Instance:

_____

_____

Response:

_____

_____

_____

Instance:

_____

_____

Response:

_____

_____

_____

Instance:

_____

_____

Response:

_____

_____

_____

Protect Yourself

Protecting ourselves is a daily activity. We do it all the time by wearing clothes that are appropriate for the weather and locking the doors to our homes when we leave. Standing up for, speaking up for, and protecting ourselves is just as important as the outward ways we protect ourselves, and it will take some practice and getting used to.

Throughout the next few days, please take opportunities to practice positive self-talk and assertiveness. It will probably feel uncomfortable if you're not familiar with this kind of self-care. When you eventually master this, you will find it hard to believe you ever tolerated less.

When you do this practice, think of the little child you once were and how you would like that child to have been treated. Consider that that child still is a part of who you are, and all of who you are deserves love, respect, and kindness. You deserve to refuse anything less.

What Brings You Joy?

This simple exercise will hopefully help you better understand who you are and what is important to you. When you find joy in art, food, nature, family, friends, or any other area, you are being kind to yourself. After being in survival mode in your relationship with a narcissist, you may no longer recognize what is joyful to you. These do not have to be monumental things—they can be everyday things, like your dog playing or the flowers growing in your front yard. It can be watching a play or a sunset. So many things can bring us joy, and it can be something that no one else understands. I have an old blanket that I adore that everyone else thinks is ugly, but it brings me joy.

Please use the space below to write down what you find joyful:

_____

_____

_____

_____

_____

_____

_____

_____

_____

Prioritizing Your Needs

You have done a lot of work in this book, and it's time to start bringing it all together. So much of this recovery you are doing is about finding out more about yourself and hopefully, at this point, you know what is most important to focus on. I strongly encourage you to start journaling so you can track your progress and remind yourself what is important to you, should you get off track. A journal and calendar are good ways to monitor where you are in your recovery and what you need. Start by creating a list of what you feel you need to attend to first. This book is laid out to help you build on the skills and information learned in the previous chapter, but you know you—depending on your own needs, it might be more important to you to start with reducing negative self-talk or another skill.

Please list what you would like to start with first, then consider scheduling time to do so each day or week by marking it in your calendar. It's helpful to journal what you do and how you feel each day as well.

Priority 1:

_____

_____

_____

Priority 2:

_____

_____

_____

Priority 3:

_____

_____

_____

Priority 4:

_____

_____

_____

Priority 5:

_____

_____

_____

A Letter to You

Please use the space here to write a little letter to yourself in appreciation of who you are and talk about how you intend to keep learning to love and care for yourself and not let anyone destroy that ever again. Note what you have accomplished through the activities in this book and what you plan to focus on in the future. Return to this letter from time to time to keep in touch with each part of yourself. Please write with the love and compassion you deserve, and no self-blaming! When you know better, you do better, and this is the time and place that both have aligned for you. You are free to write a couple of pages or use up all the space; however many lines you need to express yourself.

Dear Me,

_____

_____

_____

_____

_____

_____

_____

_____

_____

_____

_____

_____

_____

_____

Love,

Me

REAL-LIFE STORY: CARA AND JACOB

My client Cara has been with me from the beginning of her separation from her husband to their reconciliation after both of them did, and continue to do, deep work on healing with a specialist in narcissistic abuse. Cara grew up with a narcissistic father, then married Jacob, who had many narcissistic traits of his own. Cara had been through a lot of emotional abuse from Jacob, and a physical assault was the final straw for Cara. She moved out of their shared home into her own place and created strong boundaries with Jacob, which led to consequences if he did not respect them. Through a lot of hard work, Cara was able to learn to care for herself and respect the fact that she mattered just as much as Jacob did. It was not clear for a while whether reconciliation was something Cara even wanted until they started working with the specialist.

The most beautiful part of their story is how each of them has been able to face and heal from their painful pasts, and Cara has learned to love herself and trust her intuition. Their story is uplifting and unique, because most couples don't get to this point in repairing all the damage done in a narcissistic relationship. They are a testament that doing the work and not giving up when setbacks occur are worthwhile in order to reach your goals.

A Final Word

I would like to take this opportunity to applaud you. This is no easy workbook to do—nor an easy subject to face—and you have met the challenge. I commend you for taking the hard looks at yourself and making changes to improve things so you can live more freely and authentically. You have so much to be proud of and most of all, the fact that you even chose this book means that you already have some self-love and self-esteem and are practicing self-care. You have gained knowledge, information, and skills to help you on this journey that will lead to a much better quality of life than the one you have or had with a narcissist. Change takes time, and I hope you will be patient with yourself as you keep practicing what you have learned in this book. My hope is that you will return to it often to see what you wrote and remind yourself of the goals you have created and the direction you are moving toward.

A relationship with a narcissist is one that most other people do not see, even though you are suffering. It can be hard to find therapists or coaches who can walk you through the unique healing and recovery process required with this type of abuse. Fortunately, although there are still not enough therapists and other healers to work with survivors of narcissistic abuse, there are more now than I have ever seen in the past. My hope is that this number will continue to grow so that abused people can be seen and heard, and that everyone has a chance to heal and recover properly. There is nothing like talking to someone who understands the intricacies and insidiousness of narcissistic abuse. I wish you all the best on your continued journey and hope you will seek out as many resources as you can find to continue your self-discovery on your road to recovery. Stay strong, maintain your boundaries, and allow yourself time to recharge as often as needed. You've got this!

Resources

Books

There are many useful books that explore other aspects of narcissistic abuse and I encourage you to search them out. I strongly recommend: *"Don't You Know Who I Am?": How to Stay Sane in an Era of Narcissism, Entitlement, and Incivility* by Dr. Ramani S. Durvasula. In this book, she does a thorough job of explaining narcissistic behavior and how it has become so pervasive in recent years.

Websites

Narcissistic Abuse Recovery Center

NarcTrauma.com

My own practice offers many services for survivors of narcissistic abuse, so please reach out if you are interested in therapy, coaching, workshops, or groups. You can visit the NarcTrauma website or StephensTherapy.com for more information.

The National Domestic Violence Hotline

TheHotline.org

A 24/7 hotline that provides tools and support to help survivors of domestic violence so they can live their lives free of abuse. You can chat with them on their website or by phone at 1-800-799-SAFE (7233) or TTY 1-800-787-3224.

National Resource Center on Domestic Violence

VAWnet.org

VAWnet is a clearinghouse of information regarding domestic violence.

Psychology Today

PsychologyToday.com

You can use terms like "narcissistic abuse" in the search fields of this website to find a therapist who is the right fit for you.

References

Ambardar, Sheenie. 2018. "How Is Narcissistic Personality Disorder (NPD) Treated?" Medscape, May 16. Medscape.com/answers/1519417-101769/how-is-narcissistic-personality-disorder -npd-treated.

American Psychiatric Association. 2013. *Diagnostic and Statistical Manual of Mental Disorders, Fifth Edition.* Arlington, VA: American Psychiatric Publishing.

Caligor, Eve, Kenneth N. Levy, and Frank E. Yeomans. 2015. "Narcissistic Personality Disorder: Diagnostic and Clinical Challenges." *American Journal of Psychiatry* 172, no. 5 (May): 415–422. AJP.PsychiatryOnline.org/doi/10.1176/appi.ajp.2014.14060723.

Davis, Shirley. 2020. "The Neuroscience of Narcissism and Narcissistic Abuse." CPTSD and Narcissistic Abuse, CPTSD Research (June 22). CPTSDFoundation.org/2020/06/22/the -neuroscience-of-narcissism-and-narcissistic-abuse.

Durvasula, Ramani S. 2019. *"Don't You Know Who I Am?": How to Stay Sane in an Era of Narcissism, Entitlement, and Incivility.* New York: Post Hill Press.

Elise, Sophia. 2019. "Experiences of Narcissistic Abuse: An Exploration of the Effects on Women Who Have Had a Long Term, Intimate, Relationship with a Suspected Narcissistic Male Partner." Thesis for Master of Applied Practice (January). ResearchGate.net /publication/341275894.

Foster, Caroline. 2019. *Narcissistic Mothers: How to Handle a Narcissistic Parent and Recover from CPTSD.* Self-published.

Hoermann, Simone, Corrine E. Zupanick, and Mark Dombeck. n.d. "Biological Factors Related to the Development of Personality Disorders (Nature)." Gulf Bend Center. GulfBend.org /poc/view_doc.php?type=doc&id=41557&cn=8.

Hope, Amanda. 2021. *Narcissistic Mothers: A Healing Guide for Daughters with Mothers Who Can't Love. Learn How to Find Your Sense of Self, Recover After Narcissistic Abuse and Deal with Toxic Parents.* Self-published.

Howard, Vickie. 2019. "Recognising Narcissistic Abuse and the Implications for Mental Health Nursing Practice." *Issues in Mental Health Nursing* 40, no. 8 (August): 644–654. doi.org /10.1080/01612840.2019.1590485.

Howes, Satoris S., Edgar E. Kausel, Alexander T. Jackson, and Jochen Reb. 2020. "When and Why Narcissists Exhibit Greater Hindsight Bias and Less Perceived Learning." Journals. Sagepub.com/doi/abs/10.1177/0149206320929421

Lee, Royce J., David Gozal, Emil F. Coccaro, and Jennifer Fanning. 2020. "Narcissistic and Borderline Personality Disorders: Relationship with Oxidative Stress." *Journal of Personality Disorders* 34, Supplement (March): 6–24. GuilfordJournals.com/doi/10.1521/pedi.2020.34.supp.6.

Malkin, Mallory Laine. 2014. "Differences in Narcissistic Presentation in Abused and Non-Abused Children and Adolescents." University of Southern Mississippi Dissertations (August). Aquila.USM.edu/dissertations/274.

Michigan State University. 2019. "Me, Me, Me! How Narcissism Changes throughout Life." ScienceDaily (December 10). ScienceDaily.com/releases/2019/12/191210111655.htm.

Stephens, Brenda. 2021. *Recovering from Narcissistic Mothers: A Daughter's Guide*. Emeryville, CA: Rockridge Press.

Stinson, Frederick S., Deborah A. Dawson, Risë B. Goldstein, S. Patricia Chou, Boji Huang, Sharon M. Smith, et al. 2008. "Prevalence, Correlates, Disability, and Comorbidity of DSM-IV Narcissistic Personality Disorder: Results from the Wave 2 National Epidemiologic Survey on Alcohol and Related Conditions." *The Journal of Clinical Psychiatry* 69, no. 7 (July): 1033–1045. doi.org/10.4088/jcp.v69n0701.

Valashjardi, Ava and Kathy Charles. 2019. "Voicing the Victims of Narcissistic Partners: A Qualitative Analysis of Responses to Narcissistic Injury and Self-Esteem Regulation." *SAGE Open* (April 28): 1–10. Journals.SagePub.com/doi/10.1177/2158244019846693.

Vaknin, Sam. 2020. "Dissociation and Confabulation in Narcissistic Disorders." *Journal of Addiction and Addictive Disorders* (March). doi: 10.24966/AAD-7276/100039.

Index

Acknowledgments

The clients I have had the privilege to serve have made it possible for me to write about narcissistic abuse. In my practice as a therapist and a coach, I noticed how many more people were coming for help in dealing with strikingly similar relationship problems. Through my own experience and from the clients who have allowed me to walk with them on their healing journeys, I have been able to understand narcissistic abuse thoroughly and see how prevalent it is.

I am grateful for others in the helping professions who serve victims of narcissistic abuse and their willingness to collaborate and share their wisdom with other helping professions to understand this unique and insidious type of abuse so that more of us are able to support people who have been abused.

About the Author

 **Brenda Stephens** is a therapist and coach who works with survivors of narcissistic abuse, complex PTSD, and trauma. She is the author of *Recovering from Narcissistic Mothers: A Daughter's Guide*. Brenda is the founder of a group practice in Southern California and a coaching practice, the Narcissistic Abuse Recovery Center (NarcTrauma.com), assisting survivors of narcissistic abuse globally. She offers training to other therapists in an attempt to increase the number of healers available to people suffering from this type of abuse.